THE ART OF
TRANSLATION

THEODORE SAVORY

THE ART OF
TRANSLATION

Nec verbum verbo curabis reddere fidus
Interpres

HORACE

Publishers THE WRITER, INC. *Boston*

FIRST AMERICAN EDITION PUBLISHED BY
THE WRITER, INC., 1968
THIS EDITION © 1968 BY THEODORE SAVORY

LIBRARY OF CONGRESS CATALOG CARD NUMBER 68-15399

PRINTED IN GREAT BRITAIN

TIBI
ITERUM
CARISSIMAE
LIBRUM DEDICAVI MEUM
AMORIS PIGNUS AETERNI

It sounded wonderful in Greek,
    Translation robbed it of its magic;
Although that tongue I do not speak
It sounded wonderful in Greek.
Yet, while the cause in vain I seek
    For this metempsychosis tragic,
It sounded wonderful in Greek —
    Translation robbed it of its magic.

Evelyn Lambart

CONTENTS

PREFACE TO THE FIRST EDITION

No one who is interested in language can for long confine his interest to his native language only, and from the moment that his thoughts are turned to the words and phrases used in other countries he is brought face to face with the problems of translation. Almost as soon as he begins to realize the nature of these problems he is likely to find himself ensnared by their fascination.

Their attractiveness lies in their intractability, in the varied attempts that men have made to overcome the difficulties that translation offers and in the absence of any final and universally accepted solutions.

When I began to consider these things I was surprised by the comparatively small amount of critical attention they have received. Translations are many, almost beyond the counting, but appraisals of the art of the translator are in proportion fewer. A scientist of today, compiling for himself a literature-list of the matter on which he is engaged, may reasonably expect to find some scores of titles in his bibliography; the student of the process of translation is unlikely to come upon a couple of dozen. To these there must be added a large number of suggestions and statements, brief or not so brief, contained in Prefaces and Introductions to translated books, in which the writer has expounded his ideas of the business and has explained the principles that he has adopted for guidance. Two features of these paragraphs have helped, to my mind, to justify the present book; and these are, first, the fact that translators have freely contradicted one another about almost every aspect of their art; and, secondly, that they have written as if all translation were the conversion of a literary masterpiece in one language into a literary achievement in another. This is so manifestly untrue that it almost demands an attempt to provide a more balanced treatment, such as might be found in a Treatise on Translation. This book is not a treatise, but it is planned on the lines, if not on the scale, of one.

I am greatly indebted to my eldest sister for her wise criticisms, suggestions and encouragement, and to my friend and colleague Mr David Small for his ready help. I would also express my thanks to a number of correspondents, including Miss A. Munro-Kerr of the Society of Authors, Mr Oliver Edwards of *The Times*, Mr R. J. Evans, Mr John Hampden of the British Council, and Dr J. E. Holmstrom of UNESCO. I would also thank Mrs Mary Brown for her help in preparing the typescript.

1957   T. H. S.

PREFACE TO THE SECOND EDITION

The warm appreciation which this book received on its first appearance was a surprise to its author. I received an unexpected number of letters from unknown writers who were evidently interested in what I had written, and many of these sent me very valuable information and some valued comments. Although I personally answered every letter at the time, I must again express my gratitude for their contributions, which have provided a considerable part of the modifications to be found in the present edition.

I must also record my appreciation of E. Cary's work, *La Traduction dans le Monde Moderne*, and acknowledge my debt to Professor J. J. Bruce's magnificent book on *The English Bible*, which has caused me entirely to rewrite Chapter VIII.

For the rest there will be found certain amplifications and additions consequent upon ideas that have come my way during the past decade, most of which time, I ought to admit, has been devoted not to letters but to zoology.

Finally I should like to thank Mr George Walker for permission to reprint the correct version of his incomparable 'Papa joue au cricket', and Mr Peter Davis of Luxembourg for his stimulating correspondence; and especially my friends Mrs Mary Stirling, Mr G. C. F. Mead, and Dr Julian Verbov for their ready response to my appeals for help. The passage from C. Day Lewis's *Aeneid* (Copyright 1952 by C. Day Lewis), and that from Angela Thirkell's *Summer Half*, are reprinted here by kind permission of the Harold Matson Co. Inc. and Alfred A. Knopf respectively.

1968   T. H. S.

I

Some fundamentals

Go to, let us go down, and there confound their language, that they may not understand one another's speech.

GEN. xi, 7

The story of Babel relates, in the form of a legend, the origin of a constraint imposed upon the human race from the early days of its evolution. Although the power to communicate with others is no longer regarded as a characteristically human achievement for which no other animal possesses the capacity, the habit of speaking in different languages is peculiar to Man. Thus there has arisen a situation that is biologically unique, the existence of a species in which some individuals are unable to understand the words and expressions of some other individuals. This phenomenon creates a barrier to intercourse which is encountered whenever men try to communicate with one another across a great distance of space or across a great interval of time. Something has to be done to overcome this restriction, for we are paying a high price for the luxury of speaking in different tongues.

Translation, the surmounting of the obstacle, is made possible by an equivalence of thought that lies behind its different verbal expressions. No doubt this equivalence is traceable to the fact that men of all nations belong to the same species. When an Englishman is thinking of the woman whom he describes as 'my mother', another will be thinking of *ma mère*, or of *meine Mutter* or of *mi madre*, and among normal people their thoughts will be very similar and will recall the same memories of tenderness, loving care and maternal

13

pride. In consequence 'my mother' can be perfectly translated by any one of the three alternatives just given.

A collection of sufficient examples of this kind of equivalence in thought will produce a list of French or German or Spanish words, that is to say a French or German or Spanish vocabulary. Repetition of the process, adequately continued, will produce a French or a German or a Spanish dictionary. Why then is translation so often considered to be difficult? Are there not dictionaries in plenty — most interesting books which are useful to many and to translators invaluable?

The answers to these questions can be given when it is realized that the idea that lies behind the nature of a dictionary of the x = y type is essentially fallacious. Any good dictionary demonstrates this fact. The notion that for every word in any one language there is another word accurately equivalent to it in every other language, is not in accordance with experience; moreover, the belief, admittedly excusable, that two words with the same, or with nearly the same, spelling, but belonging to different languages, must have the same meaning is even further from the truth. Indeed, as we all know, a good dictionary tacitly admits this fact by offering its readers two, three or more 'translations' for any word about which he consults its pages; and the reader is left to choose, as well as he can, the one that best suits his purpose. In his search for the equivalent of a word the translator meets many difficulties; and here at the very beginning of a discussion of the whole subject of translation some of the most obvious of these difficulties may not unreasonably be considered. This will help to put the act of translation into a true perspective and to define the attitude of the translator in relation to his work, as well as providing a foundation on which to build the rest of our argument.

The commonest pitfall that lies in the path of the student, and is always waiting to trap him even when, later, his experience is wider, has been described by the high-sounding name of 'illusory correspondence', or, more poetically, as 'false friends'. The student reads *luridi flores*, and, without pausing to think, translates by the words 'lurid flowers'. Difficulties of this kind should not be regarded as serious, because they are no more than the consequence of the translator's negligence. The dictionary, had he consulted it, would have given him 'yellow' as the first equivalent of *luridus*; and a translator has no excuse for omitting to use his dictionary.

But let this be looked at in reverse. Required to translate 'yellow flowers' into Latin, a writer would probably choose the adjective *flavus* rather than *luridus*, and this because *flavus* is more generally used in such poetic relations as flowers suggest. It is commonly to be found in the phrase *flavum aurum*, yellow gold, and more often in *coma flava*, yellow hair, or, as we should be more inclined to say, golden hair. There is an implication of shining lustre about the word *flavus*, which it has acquired by reason of the contexts in which it was used by Virgil and Horace. What of *luridus*? No bright lustre is suggested here, the implication is the reverse: pale yellow in mild cases, wan or even gloomy in others. 'Smeared with gore and ghastly pale,' wrote Gray in *The Bard*, and *luridus* is the equivalent of his last two words. If it be permissible to migrate for a moment from the world of literature to that of botany, it may be said that to the botanist *flavi flores* suggests carotin and xanthophyll, while *luridi flores* suggests etiolin. In fact, neither *flavus* nor *luridus* can be said simply and indifferently to mean 'yellow'.

The translator, therefore, can avoid the mistake of this illusory equivalence only if he has some feeling for the accrued implications of a word, or, as they are usually called, for its associations. Two words which belong to different languages and yet have the same spelling must, at some time, have been the same word. They may be different now because many writers in the two languages have used them differently. I myself have retained for years the memory of an occasion when, visiting a Malvern friend, I looked from his study window at the matchless beauty of the Vale of Evesham, spreading before us in the summer sunshine. I tried, with faltering phrase, to say something worthy of the scene. 'Yes,' he said, 'I have always thought that this view comes nearer to the Latin word *splendidus* than anything else I know.' I suppose that there is more education to be had from that remark than from an hour's reading of Ovid; it would scarcely be possible to find a more incisive way of learning that *splendidus* cannot just be said to mean 'splendid'.

Troubles of a different kind arise from gaps in languages, which cannot be filled by translating because for a word that may be quite familiar in one language there is no equivalent in another. Probably the first example that will occur to many is the failure of French to provide a word for 'home'. 'I shall go home,' says the Englishman; and the Frenchman: '*J'irai chez moi*.' 'This is my home,' says the Englishman on arrival; but the Frenchman can get no nearer than *Voilà ma maison*, or *mon logis* or *ma demeure*, all words whose primary significance is that contained in the Englishman's 'house' or 'residence'. So, too, there is no English word for the French *menu* or for the Latin word *augur* and no Latin word for the English word 'premier'.

Difficulties of this kind are frequent in the translation of all kinds of writings where the two nations whose languages are concerned may have different customs, different games and amusements, and different degrees of technical development. A phrase such as 'two strings to one's bow' can be put into almost any other language because archery has for long been practised over almost the whole of the world; it is nearly impossible to put 'better than a yard' into the language of any nation that has never known royal tennis. The habit of five o'clock tea was introduced by the English to the French, whose language had no word for such a meal. It accordingly became known as *le fiveocloque*, and this gave rise to a corresponding verb, so that at one time one might read in a hotel the information that '*On fivocloque à quatre heures*'. More recently the terms *le snack-bar* and *le self-service* may be seen. In technical translation the problems are more obvious. Open-cast coal-mining, for example, is a peculiarly English atrocity, and to name it adequately in French requires thought and imagination as well as a good knowledge of the language.

Idioms and idiomatic phrases provide clear-cut difficulties which every translator very soon meets.

'A widow lives in sleepy Chester' is a plain statement, which can be easily translated into Spanish, Bulgarian or any other ordinary language; but the first line of Kipling's poem is: 'There's a widow in sleepy Chester'. The idiom 'there is', one of the commonest idioms in English, would be represented in French by *Il y a* and in German by *Es gibt*, which literally seem to mean something quite different. More difficulties are thus introduced, and the way out of them can be found only by experience. *Il n'y a pas de quoi* does not stand for 'He there has not of what', but how is anyone to guess that it means 'It does not matter'?

Idiomatic and other peculiar forms of expression are to a recognizable extent the products of the national characteristics, which in themselves do nothing to make the work of the translator easier. '*Mon Dieu*,' said a Frenchman in *Punch* many years ago, '*c'est magnifique, superbe, c'est* ... what you Engleesh call "*pas demi mauvais*"!' No doubt he was correct, and the bathos was justifiable, but the would-be translator, who remembers the anecdote, finds that his burden is the heavier. The next time that his reading includes some phrases of extravagant admiration, he is compelled to pause and to ask himself whether they should not be rendered by the words 'not half bad'.

Much the same difficulty may be found with proverbial expressions. *Mit Wölfen muss man heulen* seems to be a straightforward statement and a translator may write 'Among wolves one must howl'. The critic then says, 'That is nonsense, isn't it? You should have written "When in Rome, do as Rome does".' The translator replies, 'But that is not what the author wrote.' 'No,' says the critic, 'but it is what he meant.' And so the translator faces the question as to whether his function is to record the words of his original author or to give their meaning.

Although the elementary difficulties outlined above are likely to occur in making translations of all kinds, there are also difficulties that are characteristic of translations of particular kinds. This introduces a fact of an importance that cannot be overstressed. A very large part of the existing writings on the subject of translation treat it as though it were a uniform process, and nearly always as though it consisted only of the translation of Latin and Greek poetry into English verse; whereas translation is a many-sided art, and no balanced or proportionate study of it can neglect this fact. This complexity in the character of translation underlies much of the treatment given to it in this book, and the point should be considered more fully here. Four different categories of translation will be recognized.

Yet before the enumeration of these is begun, reference may be made to instances and circumstances where translation is unnecessary and, in fact, is not made. For an example one may choose the homely fact that at one time it was the custom at important lawn tennis matches in France for the umpire to call out the scores in English. The scores in lawn tennis are counted, as readers are no doubt aware, as 'love', 'fifteen', 'thirty', 'forty', and 'game'. Into the reasons why nought is called 'love', why the first two points are rated at fifteen units each, the third at ten, and the fourth at no specified number no inquiry is necessary, for the essence of the position is that it demonstrates very clearly that the words used are symbols to which a significance has been attached arbitrarily, or by arrangement, or perhaps by tradition. In this case the meaning is arbitrary, since the words used represent each quarter of the course of a normal game. They could be replaced by any other set of sounds, such as one, two, three, and four, or ack, beer, see, and don: and for this reason nothing would be gained by replacing them by *quinze, trente, quarante,* and *jeu.* That this has not been done is a tacit recognition of the principle, which this paragraph emphasizes, that a word is nothing more than a symbol with a traditional meaning. Nothing connects the words *Hund, chien, perro, cane,* or 'dog' with the familiar animal except long-standing custom, by which the symbol or word is accepted as a representation of the idea.

Here at once we run up against the mathematical consequence that more ideas are generated by human minds than there are words with which to give them utterance. This situation is met, and can only be met, in two ways: one is by inventing new words, the normal method of the child in the nursery and the scientist in the laboratory; the other is to force some words to carry a double or a multiple burden, and so to be responsible for more ideas or things than one. Thus the English word 'square' may appear in French as *carré* (square-shaped), *juste* or *vrai* (honest), *place* (Trafalgar Square), *équerre* (carpenter's instrument), *égaliser* (to make square), as well as in a variety of phrases such as 'to get square with', or as the alternative to 'egg-head'.

No discussion of translating can have any meaning unless this fact is continuously, if subconsciously, in mind.

The categories of translation, mentioned above, must now be characterized.

I. All purely informative statements, such as are encountered by the traveller or used by the advertiser. For example, at some air terminals there hang notice boards inscribed with the following messages:

IMPORTANT
Please ensure that your baggage is correct before leaving the air terminus.

ATTENTION
Messieurs les passagers sont priés de vérifier leurs bagages avant de quitter l'aérogare.

ACHTUNG
Überzeugen Sie sich bitte, dass Sie Ihr eigenes Gepäck haben, bevor Sie dieses Gebäude verlassen.

IMPORTANTE
Se ruega a los señores pasajeros controlen su equipaje antes de salir de esta estación terminal.

The probability is that each anxious or hurried traveller reads only one of these, according to his nationality; but a visitor to the air-station, who sits awaiting his friend's arrival, may study them all and will easily perceive their obvious characteristic. The four messages are not word for word identically phrased, but all contain advice of identical meaning. One may assume that an Englishman, a Frenchman, a German, and a Spaniard take away exactly the same impressions, and that they all usually react in the same way and possibly with the same sensations. In other words, here is perfect translation. No critic is likely to cavil at any word in any of the three notices; and, if he does so, he may find it hard to sustain his objection.

Clearly enough, the perfection of the translation is a result of the nature of the original message. It is direct and unemotional and it is made in plain words to which no very intense associations are attached. Probably, therefore, the translations were very easily made, without very much hesitation on the part of the translator. The best words available to take the places of 'ensure', 'baggage' and 'leaving' were ready to hand, and the translator, whoever he was, no doubt felt quite certain that his sentences would be correctly understood by his readers, whoever they were.

In this he was right, and his success in translating is important to students of the subject. It proves that in some circumstances perfect translation is a possibility. So much of the discussion about translation arises from the impossibility of perfectly translating many kinds of writing that an admission that perfection is attainable is of value, and helps us to define the rare conditions in which it is to be found.

II. From the perfect we proceed to the adequate; to translations that are so satisfactory in practice that a grumble at words or phrases here and there may be dismissed as a quibble. Into this second category fall the very large number of almost characterless translations made 'for the general reader', who may use them without giving a thought to the fact that what he is reading was not originally written in his own language. All the ordinary readers of all the translations of Dumas's *Black Tulip*, Boccaccio's *Decameron*, Cervantes's *Don Quixote*, and Tolstoy's *Anna Karenina* and so on, have brought this category into existence.

Clearly, in most instances of this kind the readers may know little or nothing of the language of the original, and may possibly have no interest at all in such linguistic problems as translation abundantly raises; so that the translator, realizing this, is justified in wasting no time in deliberation over the words and phrases that he uses. He may omit words, or even whole sentences, which he finds obscure; he can freely paraphrase the original meaning whenever it suits him to do so. In other words, he is working in easy-going conditions, and this may be reflected in the version that he produces.

And, indeed, there is no reason why this should not be so, as long as the readers want nothing but the story. Obviously, a young undergraduate does not devour an unexpurgated copy of *The Decameron* because of any interest in the Italian language or in Italian literature, but because he is anxious to read of the behaviour of the nightingale and of other characters in a book which at intervals disturbs self-constituted guardians of public morals. To turn ordinary readable prose that has no outstanding characteristics, and makes no claim to be great literature, from one language to another, producing a version that is also ordinary, readable, and unambitious, is not, in general, a very interesting process; nor, in consequence, is it often that anything of very great interest can be said about it, whether as criticism, comment, or commendation. Yet I am assured by a former pupil, now occupied in such work, that translations of this nature are largely what both publishers and the public seem to appreciate.

All this is but another way of saying that, both in the original and the translation, the matter is more important than the manner, and so foreshadows the nature of our third category. This includes the translation of all forms of writing in which the manner is at least as important as the matter, and may far surpass it: in other words, the translation of literature, made by scholars for serious students, and for all earnest readers who are seeking as they read something more than mere entertainment.

III. This third category is a composite one, including, as it does, the translation of prose into prose, of poetry into prose, and of poetry into poetry. It thus embraces almost the whole of the translations which in the past have so appealed both to translators and their critics that around them the commentaries and discussions on the art of translation have arisen.

In this category only can the theoretical impossibility of perfect translation have so serious an effect that the conscientious translator may spend a very long time on his work. The time may, indeed, be so long that the commercial value of the translation is wholly neglected, and all that is gained is the intellectual exercise and the keen intellectual pleasure that results from the effort. A great quantity of translation is, in fact, made, printed and published for no other reason than this, that the translator has enjoyed the reading of some passage or poem, has felt the urge to try to render or express it in English, and has fallen under the spell of the task to such a degree that he has wished to share his pleasure with others.

Further, in this category there must be included all the first-quality translations of the literature of Greece and Rome, a very long series of scholarly works which have appeared in an uninterrupted stream ever since the Elizabethan age. One of the few features of modern life that is really heartening to the lover of scholarship is the continuing publication today of translations of this kind.

IV. In the fourth and last category is included the translation of all learned, scientific and technical matter. Translators of this kind of material may appear not to be very different from those in the second category, in which perhaps they might have been included as a special sub-group; and certainly in them the matter is of the first importance and the manner of no significance whatever. Scientific and technical translating has, however, certain characteristics of its own.

First, these translations are made solely because of the intrinsic importance of the original work, an importance that is strictly confined to the practical business of living. Professor R. C. Punnett's *Mendelism* was translated into Japanese only because the Japanese needed to know the principles of heredity; and it may well be that not a single reader in Tokyo derived from his study of the translation any impression of the accuracy, clearness and precision with which, as I so well remember, Punnett wrote and lectured in the English language.

Again, scientific and technical translation is peculiar in that it is almost a necessity that the translator shall have a reasonable knowledge of the science or technique about which the original was written. Whereas a translator of the *Anabasis* needs little more than a knowledge of Greek, a translator of a foreign geological text must know some geology. Without it his work would scarcely be possible.

This fourth category must also be held to include the vast quantity of translation work done solely in the interests of trade. Manufactured objects, often known as 'consumer goods', can be sold in countries other than those in which they were made only if they can be persuasively described in the language of the purchasers. The work of the linguists who perform this service in the interests of Mammon is seldom publicized, seldom appreciated, seldom criticized. Yet, particularly from their own point of view, their work demands accuracy in the choice and precision in the use of words which many other translators might find to be more than they could endure.

There is yet one further type of translating which is altogether omitted from this book, not by accidental oversight but on purpose. This is the work of the interpreter. The omission does not imply any lack of appreciation of the interpreter's skill, which is always impressive and often amazing. But the spoken word, produced spontaneously and almost, as it seems, instinctively, must undeniably represent a human achievement of a wholly different genre from the slower, painstaking thought that results in the written and published translation.

II

The work of translation

All translation is a compromise — the effort to be literal and the effort to be idiomatic.

BENJAMIN JOWETT

At all times and in all places translations have been made for purely utilitarian purposes and with no other thought in the mind of the translator than to remove the barrier that is placed, by a difference in languages, between the writer and the reader.

'And a superscription also was written over him in letters of Greek, and Latin, and Hebrew ...'

The words of St Luke recall one of the best-known references to solely informative translation.

This is the primitive state of translation and, like that of a primitive animal, it is a state from which more elaborate, more specialized forms are destined to develop or evolve.

Verae amicitiae sempiternae sunt.
True friendships are everlasting.

That is a perfect example of primitive translation, verbally accurate, yet lacking in any other quality for which it may be commended. As soon as a translator is required to produce a rendering different from and better than this, he faces all the problems involved in the choosing of words.

Consider such a simple and not unfamiliar sentence as

Quo facto, Caesar ad castra rediit.

For the advantage of a beginner this might be translated as

25

'Which having been done, Caesar returned to the camp'. But this is not normal English, and an improvement might be 'When this was done, Caesar returned to the camp'. This may reasonably be expected to remind the reader of the Ablative Absolute: but a reader who had never opened a Latin book might prefer 'After this, Caesar returned to camp', while for one who can read the original if he wishes a fourth possibility is 'Afterwards Caesar rode back to camp'.

This example proves that the translator's task is much harder than that of the original author. When the latter seeks a word with which to express a thought or describe an experience, he has available many words in his own language, and can without great difficulty or delay choose the one that suits him best and pleases him most. The translator of the word thus chosen has to decide on the nearest equivalent, taking into consideration the probable thoughts of the author, the probable thoughts of the author's readers and of his own readers, and the period of history in which the author lived.

Hence at every pause the translator makes a choice; and from what has been said in the first chapter about the correspondence of words, his choice is clearly not between alternative yet exact equivalents, but between a number of equivalents, all more or less inexact. Such a choice depends largely on the personality of the translator, and that it is essentially an aesthetic choice cannot be denied.

A fair conclusion from these ideas is that the translator's work may be analysed into the answering of three questions. Faced with a passage in the original language, he must ask himself:

   (i) What does the author say?
  (ii) What does he mean?
 (iii) How does he say it?

This method of analysis may be applied to the paragraph, to the sentence, or even to the phrase; and to follow its working in a simple case is illustrative of its value.

The translator reads, for example, the three words of the familiar expression *ventre à terre*, and asks the first question. There is, of course, seldom much room for doubt about the answer: any difficulty should be solved by the use of a dictionary, and here the answer is that the author says 'belly to ground'. This strikes the ear so strangely that the second question is inevitable; and the answer is that the author means 'very quickly', or perhaps 'as quickly as possible' or 'at top speed'. But the translator will not, or should not, be satisfied either with the crudeness of the first translation, or with the coldness of the second, or with the stupid adjective of the third. None of these expressions evokes the picture of horse or hound with almost horizontal legs, as is implicit in *ventre à terre*; so that the translator must ask the third question, How does he say it? Is the author writing clearly and calmly, or with some degree of emphasis, or with a compelling eloquence that will stir the uninterested and unimaginative minds of his readers? When the translator has determined the character of his author's style he is able to choose between the less emphatic 'at full stretch' and the more emphatic 'hell for leather'.

By this simple example the nature of the problem which a translator has to solve is made clear, and the alternative solutions which exist show he can exercise his choice between them. It should be followed by another well-known phrase, the Frenchman's *l'esprit de l'escalier*. How often we have recounted to a sympathetic ear the stages of some unsatisfactory discussion in which we have lately been engaged, and have been obliged to end with the confession, 'Of course afterwards I realized that I ought to have said ... ' This recognition of the way in which, too late, we might have clinched the argument is all contained in the words *l'esprit de l'escalier*. One can see the discomforted speaker retiring upstairs, uncertain that he has made the best of his case, thinking suddenly of what he might have said, and hesitating, foot on step, while he wonders if he shall go back, say it, and reopen the whole sorry business. The fortunate German may write *der Treppenwitz* and be satisfied; but in England we have no comparable phrase. To write 'the spirit of the staircase' is almost as meaningless and quite as foolish as to write 'stomach to ground' for *ventre à terre*. What, then, can the translator do? Frankly, there is no textbook answer: he can but do his best.

The existence of possible alternatives between which the translator must make his own choice is, as we have said, the essence of his art. On it depend equally his conveyance of meaning and his conveyance of style. The writing of the original author may be blunt or subtle, hesitant or fluent, sober or cheerful, majestic or paltry; and the translation may be any of these according to the wit and skill of the translator. An example which shows how one translation may miss the style of the original while another may reproduce it is given by Ritchie and Moore. It is well known to many students of French, but it is far too good not to be re-quoted here.

Victor Hugo wrote: '*La nature mêle quelquefois ses effets et ses spectacles à nos actions avec une espèce d'à-propos sombre et intelligent, comme si elle voulait nous faire réfléchir.*' Sir Lascelles Wraxall translated this as follows: 'Nature at times blends her effects and spectacles with our actions, with a species of gloomy and intelligent design, as if wishing to make us reflect.' The writers whose names we have given offer us a very different version. 'There are times when Nature matches her shows and pageants to human actions with a weird and startling fitness, as though she were a conscious intelligence, bidding us pause and ponder.'

A large part of what has to be said on the matter of faithful and free translation might be based on these three extracts.

Art, proverbially, is long, so that translation, in so far as it is an art, should be in like manner timeless, persistently reappearing as an inevitable response to stimuli felt by succeeding generations. An artist in oils or water-colour does not refrain from making a picture of Mapledurham Mill because it has been drawn and painted so many times already; he regards this fact as one more reason for his, the latest, attempt. In the same way writers have always been ready to express in their own languages passages from epigrams and couplets to epics and long books, originally written in other tongues.

An appreciation of their efforts is found in the recognition that a new translation of any important work is always acceptable, and this is true more because of the timelessness of art of all forms than because of the changes in language and literary habit. A good translation always merits a careful study, as does any other work of fine art, so that the translator's method may be discerned and his treatment of difficulties be compared with the treatment adopted by others. If this were not so, the famous translations of Thucydides by Dr Jowett and of Sophocles by Dr Jebb would never have been superseded; Samuel Butler would not have followed Alexander Pope as a translator of Homer, and Sir Desmond Lee, the Headmaster of Winchester, would not have made a new translation of Plato.

Of subsidiary importance is the fact that a fresh translation of any work of literary merit is welcomed because the existing translations sound antiquated, or are obsolescent; and this is a factor which cannot be neglected or forgotten. It is certainly one of the reasons why translations continue to appear, even if it is not the chief one. There are fashions in literature and changes in literary taste, so that a rendering of Virgil which satisfied the Elizabethans of the sixteenth century will not necessarily appeal to the Elizabethans of the twentieth. There should be small need for hesitation on the part of anyone who considers embarking on a worthwhile translation; and one of the most unmistakable signs of the literary interests and activities of the present day is the popularity and plentifulness of new translations.

Listeners to the Third Programme of the B.B.C. will scarcely need to be reminded of this. During recent years they have had the opportunity of hearing a considerable number of broadcasts of translated works, the most characteristic of which have been the translations of Greek plays by Dr Gilbert Murray. Most of these had probably been chosen for broadcasting because of the renown of the originals; they were books, poems or plays of which the 'ordinary man' might be supposed to say to himself, 'What were these "Wasps" or "Frogs" or "Acharnians" of which I have heard? Greek to me!' Thus these translations quite clearly belong to the category which Robert Browning had in mind when he translated the *Agamemnon*, as is described in Chapter V.

A more vital feature of broadcast translations has been incorporated in the B.B.C.'s occasional habit of reading the original first and following it by two or more translations by different scholars. Here the fact of translation is emphasized and becomes, indeed, the keynote of the broadcast, while the offer of more translated versions than one recognizes the important principle that for the understanding and appreciation of a passage in a strange tongue two translations are more than twice as valuable as one.

The contention that translation is an art will be admitted without hesitation by all who have ever had much experience of the work of translating: there may be others who will not so readily agree, who will say that while there is art in the work of original writing, there must be less, and there may be none, in the subsidiary task of making a translation. In reply to such critics as have not been convinced by the opening paragraphs of this chapter, and in finally establishing the claims of translation to artistic status, a sound method is to compare the task of translation in all its forms with the universally acknowledged arts of painting and drawing. They will be found to be parallel, step by step.

First, there may be compared the work of the art student and the work of the student of languages. Both are learning their job, and, while so doing, they produce results that betray the hand of inexperience. The wrong colour or the wrong thickness of line is the equivalent of the wrong word; a mistake in drawing, in perspective, is the same as a mistake in the meaning of a phrase.

In the mature categories of translation we have distinguished between the translation of prose into prose, of poetry into prose, and of poetry into poetry. The artist's analogue of the rendering of prose by prose is found in the precision of a portrait by Sir Gerald Kelly or a landscape by Constable; and these are to be placed in contrast with a portrait by Mr Graham Sutherland or a landscape by Turner, which are analogous to the translation of poetry into poetry. Alternatively, artists like Mr Spencelayh and Picasso may be said to represent the contrasting schools of thought in the business of translation, those known as the faithful and the free.

When poetry is translated into prose the greater change is of the same nature as that which may be found in the sketches of such an artist as, for example, Sir Muirhead Bone. The sense is there, the vista is there, but the music of the verse is missing and the colour of the scene is reduced to black and white. Yet a skilful translator may be able to give his readers a prose which suggests the lilt of the original just as a feeling of colour may be introduced into a pencil or charcoal sketch.

These are among the highest forms of translation, as of art, but the analogies are not exhausted. The transcription of information to air-travellers, an example of translation that was mentioned in Chapter I, is the parallel to a piece of mechanical drawing, of which perhaps the most generally familiar examples are those printed in the booklets of instructions presented to the purchaser of a new motor-car. Both aim at nothing beyond a clear, succinct statement of fact or advice.

Scientific translations are manifestly paralleled by the work of the photographer, and contain, perhaps, about the same proportion of art, as the artist understands the word. Yet both translation and photography are affected by the technical knowledge of the operator. The engraver who shows us, in the form of a print from a steel or copper plate, a scene that was painted in oils is the exact analogue of a Thomas North who gives us Plutarch's *Lives of Famous Romans* by translating the French version of Jacques Amyot.

The analogies may even be found on the lighter side. Mark Twain, in *The Jumping Frog*, complains that his story lost its appeal when it appeared in a French translation and attributes this to the peculiarities of the French language. He illustrates thus the possibilities of caricature in translation as in art, and gives us several literal translations, chosen with a touch of genius. His masterpiece is, I think: 'I no see not that that frog had nothing of better than each frog' (*Je ne vois pas que cette grenouille n'a rien de mieux que chaque grenouille*), and to this he adds the comment, 'If that isn't grammar run to seed, then I count myself no judge.' The reader cannot but agree.

A study of the qualities to be sought in a translator forms a natural corollary to these considerations. If translation is an art, what kind of a man is the artist? Such a study must be undertaken with caution, for generalization is risky in all circumstances, and, like every other body of men, translators differ among themselves and will be found to occupy the familiar classes of the good, the bad and the indifferent. The last two may perhaps be neglected as less important, but they are not less numerous.

There can be no doubt that the first quality needed in a translator is linguistic knowledge of a rather different kind from that possessed by one who can read a foreign language readily but makes no attempt to put a rendering on paper. The translator's knowledge of the translated language must be wide; it must also be critically applied so that no detail is likely to be missed. Few forms of writing are harder to criticize than one's own, which, however great may have been the pleasure it gave during composition, is liable to present an unattractive mien when later it is subjected to revision. When a translation appears to claim that its every word is justified because it reflects the skill and power of the first author, it is quite intolerable; criticism rebounds from it and must be directed to the original text in a spirit of sincere inquiry. Unless this is done, avoidable mistakes may not be detected.

Some readers may recall that Ian Hay's *First Hundred Thousand* was translated into French and was published under the name of *Les Premiers Cent Milles*. In an early chapter Lieutenant Bobby Little was advised not to try to go on active service with the 'medicine chest' to which too many fond relatives had contributed. In the French version he was told to leave behind his *médecine à poitrine*. A more critical study of the original would have avoided an almost ludicrous mistranslation.

There must obviously be more to be said on the subject of a translator's knowledge of the language he is translating, if only because without a reasonable familiarity translating cannot even begin. The truth here is the peculiar one that a deep and accurate knowledge of a foreign tongue, such as follows years of study and wide reading, may produce a very appreciable effect on the translator's use of his own language. This is near disaster. A translator's task, as we have seen, is a difficult one, and the capacity that may help to make it less so is a practical literary ability in writing his own language, and doing so in a flexible style derived from the possession of a wide English vocabulary. This ability, and especially this desirable flexibility, suffers from a prolonged immersion in a foreign syntax. The result has been described as 'translator's English'. The writer of it has been unable to break away from the original; he has acquired a habit of too nearly literal a rendering, which, while it may well be accurate, stumbles along, a captive to the unaccustomed diction of foreign speech. To the reader such a translation is unattractive.

Rare qualities, clearly, are needed in a good translator, but linguistic knowledge and literary capacity will not, by themselves, ensure the best translation. A degree of sympathy and even more a degree of familiarity with the subject of the work that is being translated are almost essential. In the translation of verse, or of any purely literary piece of prose, sympathy with the feelings of the author is naturally expected, for in the absence of such sympathy the translator is unlikely ever to have felt an inclination to undertake his task; but in the translation of informative, scientific or philosophical works knowledge of the subject makes the translating very much easier. More than this, it often ensures the avoidance of errors which ignorance would allow to pass unnoticed.

An example which makes clear the value of such familiarity came before the present writer some years ago. A paragraph in a Danish journal contained some remarks which obviously demanded consideration, and help was sought from a friend who professed a knowledge of Norwegian. One sentence was: '*Savory (1930) er ved undersøgelser over to hjulspindere kommet til*

det resultat ... ' for which the equivalent offered to me was:
'Savory (1930) from experiments with two spinning-wheels
came to this conclusion ... ' The spinning-wheels make nonsense of this, and a very slight acquaintance with the habits
of spiders would have suggested to the translator that wheel-
web-spinners was the term that ought to have been used.

A translator who adequately fufils the requirements outlined above and who is able to attain a faultless standard of
translation is obviously not to be found easily. The art of
translation ought, therefore, to be highly valued and the
translator correspondingly well rewarded for his services. But
this is not so.

The explanation is probably to be found in the curious
trait of the literary mind in all ages and in all countries, the
urge to translate. Evidently in this respect translating resembles teaching; everybody believes that it must be easy, that
he could do it if necessary, and that he is qualified to criticize
the efforts of those who practise it. In both instances these
beliefs do not long survive the test of experience; but it is
also true that bad translating, like bad teaching, is by
comparison an easy matter. The result is that the words
written by Dryden in his Preface to Ovid's *Epistles* are still
applicable to translators of all kinds: 'It seems to me that the
true reason why we have so few versions that are tolerable,
is not from the too close pursuing of the Author's Sense, but
because there are so few who have all the talents requisite
for Translation, and that there is so little Praise and so
small Encouragement for so considerable a part of Learning.'

Of the qualities needed by a translator there has never
been much doubt. Many writers have told us that a translator
must be a master of two languages, but have added that his
mastery must not be of the same sort in both tongues, for his
knowledge of the foreign language must be critical, while
that of his own must be practical. He must have some skill

in writing verse if he undertakes to translate verse into verse; and while some have said that none but a poet should translate a poet, others have said that 'a poet cannot step off his own shadow', so that his own poetic feelings must appear in place of those of his author. And then, to linguistic knowledge and literary capacity, a translator must add sympathy, insight, diligence and conscientiousness.

If all this be admitted, or at least such of it as is not self-contradictory, clearly any scholar who is capable of the work that first-class translation requires will probably prefer to direct his undoubted talents to the production of original literature.

Therefore one must ask in conclusion why anyone is ever tempted to translate anything. The critics seem to agree that the translator is undertaking a hopeless, almost an impossible task, in return for which he will not receive a proportionate reward. Yet translations appear, even when they are not invited and no suggestion of recompense has been made. When Queen Mary died in 1953 a poem to her memory, written by Mr Charles Morgan, was printed in the *Sunday Times*; and the following week the correspondence columns contained a translation of his stanzas into Latin elegiacs, composed by Dr E. A. Barber, Rector of Exeter College.

Here lies the explanation. The truth is evident that the person who benefits most from a translation is the translator; and this should be expanded to make clear that the translator's reward is the pleasure that flows from intellectual exercise. Teachers recognize, and probably regret, that no child seems ever to enjoy making a translation; readers equally recognize that many adults do. If it were not so, translation would be among the rarest of the arts.

III

Translation through the ages

Traduttori, traditori

Translation is almost as old as original authorship and has a history as honourable and as complex as that of any other branch of literature.

In Europe the first translator whose name has been recorded was the manumitted Greek slave Livius Andronicus, who in about 240 B.C. put the *Odyssey* into Latin verse. Very possibly he was not the first writer who actually made a translation, but his effort is of interest because of its long survival. Horace knew it and used it; and some fragments of it are still extant.

Later, the early Latin authors Naevius and Ennius made translations of Greek plays, particularly those of Euripides, and were in part responsible for bringing the hexameter to Rome. Cicero was a frequent translator; as also was Catullus. In fact, a general translation of Greek into Latin, and, to a smaller extent, of Latin into Greek, continued as long as there was literature to be translated and a tradition of learning to appreciate the results.

A jump of several centuries brings us to a group of translators who have a historical significance by reason of the influence they exerted on European scholarship. The rise and development of Arabian learning in the eighth and ninth centuries was inevitably founded on that of Greece, the works of whose writers were made available by a company of Syrian scholars. These came to Baghdad, where they translated the works of Aristotle, Plato, Galen, Hippocrates and others into Arabic; and the city became the site of what might almost be called a school of translation, to which Arabian scholarship was greatly indebted.

The importance of these translations extended beyond both the time and the place. In due course Arab learning declined, to be succeeded by a European interest in intellectual matters, and three centuries later the Arabian texts are found possessed of no less vitality in Spain. Here Baghdad was displaced by Toledo, where a comparable 'college of translators' was busily occupied converting Arabic manuscripts into Latin. Consequently, when a writer in the twelfth century refers to an author like Aristotle, he may in fact be thinking of a Latin translation of an Arabic translation of a Syriac translation of the Greek. A process of this kind is not a guarantee of accuracy, and it was the cause of a number of mistakes and misunderstandings.

Toledo attracted scholars to work in its libraries for more than a century. Among those who came to do so was Adelard of Bath, who translated an Arabic version of Euclid's *Principles* into Latin, and Robert de Retines, who in 1141–3 produced the first translation of the Koran. By A.D. 1200 copies of the original Greek texts were beginning to find their way to Toledo, and the desirability of making translations of them by direct study, instead of by way of a third, intermediate, language began to be recognized.

To this period, though not to Toledo, belongs the famous translation known as *Liber gestorum Barlaam et Josaphat*. The Greek original was a legendary life of Buddha, adapted to read as a Christian narrative; it had a large circle of readers in many European languages; and Barlaam and Josaphat appealed so vividly to the faithful that the Latin Church was obliged to recognize them, fictitious though they were, as saints. This was a popular description, for there was no real cultus. Their names crept into Greek writings from about

1300, and in 1584 Baronius included them in the Roman Martyrology, not knowing that they were fictitious. The whole has been described as 'perhaps the most curious result attained by any translation'.

By the twelfth century the art of translation touched heights which it may since have equalled but has never surpassed. For a very long time a large proportion of the translations that were made, or at least such as have come down to us, were translations of biblical or other religious documents. King Alfred may be said to have set the example in the tenth century, and he was followed by Alfric, and by others in Ireland, Italy and Germany. Wyclif's Bible of 1382 was followed by those of Tyndale and Coverdale, but these cannot bear comparison, from a translator's point of view, with the German Bible of Martin Luther (1483–1546). Among the far-reaching effects of this work was the establishing of an acceptable form of literary German. Not many years later there appeared the work of Jacques Amyot, bishop of Auxerre and 'prince of translators'. The great debt that English literature owes to him comes from his translation in 1559 of Plutarch's *Lives of Famous Romans,* for this was the source from which Sir Thomas North in turn made his translation in 1579, and so contributed to an appreciable extent to Shakespeare's *Coriolanus, Julius Caesar,* and *Antony and Cleopatra.*

This brings us to the British translators and, returning a little in time, to John Bourchier, Lord Berners (1467–1553). Most of his translations were from Spanish, and have retained but little interest today; but his fame securely rests on his translation of the *Chronicles* of Froissart, where he found an author whose method and material admirably suited him.

The age of the first Elizabeth was also the first great age of translation in England, even as the age of the second Elizabeth is the second such era of copious translating. The national spirit of the time, a spirit of adventure and conquest in the physical world, was reflected in the spirit of the libraries: the translators went about their work with the same ambitions, discovering new realms of literature, and bringing home new treasures of human thought. Philemon Holland, for example, looked on his achievements as conquests, and so described them. He and his contemporaries sought to display the political and civic practices of the great nations of the past, and their chief concern was with the matter of their authors rather than with their literary skill.

And so they seldom translated directly. This fundamental principle, which Toledo had established, they almost wholly neglected. Amyot served North for Plutarch, but in this respect North was far from being alone. Thucydides undoubtedly wrote his histories in Greek, which Laurentius Vallon put into Latin, which Claude de Seyssel put into French, which Thomas Nicholls put into English. This is but one example of a language-chain, where scores existed. Nicholls was a London goldsmith, and many of the Elizabethan translators had no greater academic claim to the status of scholar. But they were active-minded and alert, and their works, if marred by inaccuracies, were as robust and as exhilarating as Elizabethan life itself. Their range was wide and their accomplishments were great.

Sir Thomas North was perhaps the most famous of them all. Philemon Holland (1552–1637), who has also been mentioned, was a surgeon and was Headmaster of Coventry Grammar School: he was a classical scholar and a writer of great industry, whose translations will bear comparison with the originals. He made translations from Xenophon, Livy, Suetonius and Pliny.

Again, the Homer of George Chapman was published between 1598 and 1616, and so belongs to this period, even though it is known today only as the origin of Keats's more famous sonnet. John Florio (1553–1625) produced in 1603 his translation of Montaigne's *Essays*, a work which ranks as the equal, at least, of North's *Plutarch*. Like the latter it was appreciated, and even appropriated, by Shakespeare, who used it in *The Tempest*; and further it showed English writers for the first time something of the nature and possibilities of the essay as a literary form. Lastly, Thomas Shelton produced in 1612 the first translation of *Don Quixote*.

The seventeenth century as a whole showed nothing like the same vigour and richness in either the study or the translation of literature from other lands. Hobbes's *Thucydides* and, later, his *Homer*, have never won general approbation; and Sir Roger l'Estrange's translations from Cicero, Juvenal and Seneca are readable, but depart too widely from their originals to have retained a reputation. The same charge of inaccuracy, or unfaithfulness, can be made against John Dryden's versions of Juvenal (1693) and Virgil (1697); but in spite of this Dryden must be counted as one of the significant translators of his age.

This is because, unlike most of his predecessors, he gave much careful and critical thought to the work of translating, or perhaps it would be fairer to say that he set down the conclusions to which he came in several places in the introductions to his poems. He was thus the first to recognize and clearly to describe translation as an art, with definite principles and an underlying theory to which a translator must submit. His careful distinguishing, for example, between paraphrase and what he characteristically called metaphrase, though it may seldom be heard today, was symptomatic of his scrupulous attitude towards the words of his original author.

To this there should, however, be added the reminder that in this matter of discussing the work of a translator Dryden had been preceded by Earl Roscommon (?1633-85). His

Essay on Translated Verse, in rhymed couplets, contains much that might be noted by translators today.

Translations were numerous in the eighteenth century, where the first that claim attention were the attempts of Alexander Pope (1688–1744) and William Cowper (1731–1800) to put Homer into English verse. Pope's *Iliad* appeared between 1715 and 1720, his *Odyssey* in 1725 and 1726 and Cowper's *Odyssey* in 1791. Cowper, it will be remembered, claimed merit for having kept as close as possible to the original; but Pope had done nothing of the kind and had earned the comment, 'It is a pretty poem, Mr Pope, but you must not call it Homer.' These translations gain in interest by comparison with each other and with the German translation of J. H. Voss, whose *Odyssey* was published in 1781, the *Iliad* following in 1793. At the end of this century A. W. von Schlegel successfully translated Shakespeare into German.

In the last decade of the eighteenth century there was published one of the rare dissertations on the art of translation. The author was Alexander Fraser Tytler, Lord Woodhouselee (1747–1814), and his book, *Essay on the Principles of Translation,* appeared in 1792. Woodhouselee was born in Edinburgh and became professor of history at Edinburgh University. In 1790 he read to the Royal Society of that city some papers on the subject of translating, from which his book was developed. By mischance, Dr George Campbell, the Principal of Marischal College, Aberdeen, had published not long before *A Translation of the Four Gospels with Notes,* and prefaced this work with some statement of the theories that he had determined and used. There was risk of misunderstanding when he read in the *Essay,* which had been published anonymously, an elaboration of some of the same ideas; but Woodhouselee, acknowledging his authorship, was able to convince Dr Campbell that there had been no plagiarism. The truth was, of course, that two scholars, searching at the same time for the same principles, would be only too likely to come to some of the same conclusions.

Woodhouselee's book, which has retained its interest and much of its value to the present day, laid down three fundamentals by which any translation should be made or judged. They were:

1. A translation should give a complete transcript of the ideas of the original work.
2. The style and manner of writing should be of the same character as that of the original.
3. A translation should have all the ease of original composition.

He proceeded to illustrate these, as well as such auxiliary ideas as occurred to him, with a wealth of examples from Greek, Latin, French, Spanish and Italian, which put his book in a class by itself. His critical opinions may not all be in accordance with present-day views, but of his breadth of learning there can be no question. A hundred years later Valéry Larbaud wrote in *Sous l'invocation de Saint Jérôme* that he would leave this earth with less regret if he could be assured that his work would one day be compared with that of Lord Woodhouselee.

The translators of the nineteenth century include several great names, and among these the first to be mentioned must be Thomas Carlyle. In 1824 he translated Goethe's *Wilhelm Meister*, a work which proved to British readers that there was at least one genius among German authors, and that German literature was worthy of study. Another feature of the age was the simultaneous production of translations by Byron, Shelley and Longfellow, examples of the translation of poetry by poets, who, especially in the case of Longfellow, showed the value of poetic ability when used for this purpose.

Outstanding far beyond all these was a work which has become, perhaps, the most famous translation of all time. Edward Fitzgerald (1809–83) was already the author of several books when he felt the attraction of Spanish literature, and in 1854 published six plays of Calderón in translation. Then he turned to Persian, and, by a stroke of genius, hit upon a new and attractive form of stanza of four pentameters with an unrhymed third line. *The Rubáiyát of Omar Khayyám* was published in 1859; it was thrice revised by its translator and its popularity today is undiminished. Dr Fitzmaurice-Kelly has said of it that 'by a miracle of intrepid dexterity, a half-forgotten Persian poet is transfigured into a pessimistic English genius.' Fitzgerald's remarkable success in *Omar* has wholly overshadowed his translations of Aeschylus and Sophocles.

Almost at the same time, 1861, there appeared Matthew Arnold's essay *On Translating Homer*, a very considerable 'essay' of over sixty pages, in which Homer is not the only subject discussed. The first point that appeals to the reader is the great value of an exposition of the translating of poetry written by another poet. Throughout his pages Arnold's own poetic ability, no less than his wide knowledge of English poetry, is abundantly apparent. If, therefore, we accept the familiar description, 'poesie into poesie', we must recognize the interest of all Arnold's opinions. No other acknowledged English poet, not even Dryden, has so fully or so clearly expressed his own views on the art of translation.

The thesis which Arnold develops is expressed thus: that a translation should affect us in the same way as the original may be supposed to have affected its first readers. This implies that, like Fitzgerald, he would sacrifice verbal accuracy for aesthetic effect. He admits that no one knows now how Homer affected the Greeks, and offers a practical test which will overcome this, namely that the translation should give to those who both know Greek and have an appreciation of poetry the same sensation as does the original. All Arnold's theory, coupled with his illustrative examples, is worth studying.

His essay loses some of its appeal because it is also a sustained criticism of a translation of Homer made by Professor F. W. Newman, brother of Cardinal Newman. Newman's theory of translation was the exact opposite of Arnold's; he wished for verbal exactitude and a continuous impression that the translation was a translation and not an original composition. Hence both Arnold's 'essay' and Newman's 'reply' introduce an air of controversy which is unwelcome and rather unhelpful. It is also rather futile, for two artists of differing temperaments cannot instruct each other how they ought to go about their businesses. One cannot imagine two poets telling each other how best to write a lyric, especially if one of them by choice wrote drama and the other epics. When, as one reads, one gets the impression that Newman can have done nothing right, one is apt to lose sight of the value of Arnold's thought.

The years of the first half of the twentieth century which were not devoted to the waging of wars or to the recovery from so doing, saw translations flowing in a broad and vigorous stream from the pens of scholars of every kind. At first the quality of many of these translations was not as high as the scholarship of the age might reasonably have demanded; they seemed to be uninspired, and in too many instances were describable as hackwork. It seemed as if many mediocre writers had discovered, and were exploiting, the regrettable fact that indifferent translation is easily achieved and is able to satisfy a multitude of uncritical readers. Even so, a debt is owing to those translators who realized that a literature had developed, or was developing, in countries whose languages were unfamiliar; and that students and lovers of literature ran a risk of being unaware of this. Russia, to take an obvious example, had a great tradition of native novelists and only a few people outside the U.S.S.R. can have read the works of Tolstoy or Dostoevsky other than in translations. And it is only because of translation that the dramas of Chekhov, Strindberg and Ibsen have had such a conspicuous influence on the modern stage.

Yet with all this there were gaps, and Ritchie and Moore, writing in 1919, were obliged to say that anyone who relied on translations could get but a very inadequate idea of contemporary French literature. One might add that comparable ideas of the literature of other countries would have been vestigial.

There were, admittedly, a number of translated works that had become so well known in Britain that they might claim consideration from students of English literature. Such were *Struwwelpeter*, which as a work of translation has been seriously compared with Fitzgerald's *Omar*, *The Arabian Nights*, *The Three Musketeers*, the fairy tales of Grimm and Andersen, *The Adventures of Baron Munchausen*, *Faust*, *Rabelais*, and *Don Quixote*. These are all translations which, in the jargon of today, would be described as integrated immigrants.

Any student of English literature is a student of literature in general and the world's great books must be known to him. From the period under consideration the work in this field of C. K. Scott Moncrieff and the collaboration of Eden and Cedar Paul stands out conspicuously and must have acted as example and inspiration to later years.

Steadily the position improved, and Bodmer wrote later, 'American and British publishers scour the Continent for translation rights of new authors.' Even a superficial study of the literary review-pages of newspapers and magazines reveals the publication of ambitious, scholarly translations of all kinds: undeniably there exists a genuine desire to know more and more about contemporary foreign literature.

In addition there is a strong interest in classical literature. In the Welfare State the ability to read Latin becomes rarer and rarer as each generation of boys and girls leaves the secondary schools, and knowledge of Greek is but a vestigial survival; and yet translations of Homer and Xenophon, of Caesar and Virgil are welcomed. This interest is almost a phenomenon; certainly it is one of the more surprising characteristics of the age. To explain it we may turn first to the B.B.C., whose Third Programme has introduced great numbers of listeners to works whose attractiveness they had earlier been unable even to suspect.

Forty, even thirty years ago no publisher could for a moment have considered the production of large numbers of translated works in cheap paperback format: yet the miracle has happened. A contemporary Penguin catalogue lists 23 titles translated from the French, 31 from Greek, 21 from Latin, 15 from Russian, and 44 from other languages, a total of 134. Here is a small library, obtainable at so reasonable a cost that the rising spiral seems to have reversed a coil or two in the interests of pure intellectual pleasures.

The description of the present as the Golden Age of translators is by no means an exaggeration, and it can be justified by a reading of Edmond Cary's *La traduction dans le monde moderne*, where many statistics support the contention. In the writing of history the mistake of carrying the narrative too close to the present is one that should be avoided by any author, but the situation in this instance is too significant to be neglected completely. My solution of the problem is provided by a perusal of the literary columns of the Press, where 'honourable mention' has been accorded to many translators of the highest standard. It is of interest to note that many of these are recognized poets. Without

47

comment or comparison I list their names in alphabetical order:

William Arrowsmith	C. Day Lewis
G. L. Bickersteth	Christopher Logue
Roy Campbell	Robert Lowell
J. M. Cohen	F. L. Lucas
Dudley Fitts	Louis Macneice
Robert Fitzgerald	W. S. Merwin
Constance Garnett	Marianne Moore
S. Gilbert	J. B. Phillips
Robert Graves	Ezra Pound
Horace Gregory	E. V. Rieu
Gerard Hopkins	Stephen Spender
Rolfe Humphries	Eric Sutton
Bertram Jessup	Arthur Waley
Richmond Lattimore	Rex Warner
J. B. Leishman	Richard Wilbur

The gratitude which the world of letters owes to them is immense; one hopes that they all receive the just reward of their labours. But whether or not, this is an exciting time to be a translator, with a lively interest in both the theoretical and practical aspects of the art. Long may it continue.

The principles of translation

True translation is a metempsychosis.
WILAMOWITZ

The artist, practise what he may, is never without his mentors, who are anxious to tell him what he ought to do, or his critics, who are as ready to tell him how he has done it. If, therefore, the proposition that translation is an art may be assumed in our opening chapters to have been established, translators must expect themselves to be subject to instruction, advice, correction and comment from all the three classes of persons who delight in offering these things – the informed, the uninformed, and the misinformed. Yet none of these three types of persons, not even the last and most dangerous, can continue to raise their voices with the sustained confidence that characterizes them all unless they hold certain illuminating principles, in the light of which they speak. These principles now invite our attention. Can they, from the mass of words they have provoked, be disinterred, recognizably enunciated, and justified?

The answer to this question is that a statement of the principles of translation in succinct form is impossible, and that a statement in any form is more difficult than might be imagined; and further that this difficulty has arisen from the writings of the translators themselves. The truth is that there are no universally accepted principles of translation, because the only people who are qualified to formulate them have never agreed among themselves, but have so often and for so long contradicted each other that they have bequeathed to us a volume of confused thought which must be hard to parallel in other fields of literature.

To make plain the nature of the instructions which would-be translators have received, a convenient method is to state them shortly in contrasting pairs, as follows:

1. A translation must give the words of the original.
2. A translation must give the ideas of the original.
3. A translation should read like an original work.
4. A translation should read like a translation.
5. A translation should reflect the style of the original.
6. A translation should possess the style of the translator.
7. A translation should read as a contemporary of the original.
8. A translation should read as a contemporary of the translator.
9. A translation may add to or omit from the original.
10. A translation may never add to or omit from the original.
11. A translation of verse should be in prose.
12. A translation of verse should be in verse.

While some of these are clearly modifications or sub-divisions of others, there is nevertheless a sufficient richness of choice to give the would-be translator a cause for embarrassment and bewilderment. The last two pairs of alternatives will be reserved for consideration in Chapter VI, after some attempt has been made to understand the existence of the rest. The very fact of their existence is in itself a real phenomenon for which an explanation must be sought; if it can be found it is likely to shed some light on the business of translation in general.

The pair of alternatives at the head of the list given above can be easily recognized as giving one form of expression to the distinction between the literal or faithful translation and the idiomatic or free translation. There has always been support for the translation which is as literal as it can well be made, support based on the conception that it is the duty of a translator to be faithful to his original. A translator, no less than any other writer, would not wish to incur the charge of being unfaithful; but before he can be certain of escaping this, he must have clearly in mind what faithfulness implies and in what faithfulness consists. It does not mean a literal, a word-for-word translation, for this is the most primitive type of translating, fit only for the most mundane and prosaic of matters; and even if faithfulness could be taken to mean this, there would remain the unavoidable fact that any one word in any language cannot invariably be translated by the same word in any other language. Most of us have read something of a man who was always described as *pius Aeneas*, and while we were quite sure that the adjective could not be translated by 'pious', we were equally sure that no one English word could properly be offered as its equivalent in every context.

One reason for the advocacy of faithfulness is that the translator has never allowed himself to forget that he is a translator. He is not, he recognizes, the original author, and the work in hand was never his own; he is an interpreter, one whose duty is to act as a bridge or channel between the mind of the author and the minds of his readers. He must efface himself and allow Rome or Berlin to speak directly to London or Paris. If he feels that he has done this, he may well be proud of his achievement. 'My chief boast,' said William Cowper, in writing of his *Homer*, 'is that I have adhered closely to the original.'

But the translator who attempts to follow this principle soon runs into difficulties, which have never been better described than in the words of Rossetti.

The work of the translator (and with all humility be it

51

spoken) is one of some self-denial. Often he would avail himself of any special grace of his own idiom and epoch, if only his will belonged to him; often would some cadence serve him but for his author's structure – some structure but for his author's cadence ... Now he would slight the matter for the music, and now the music for the matter, but no, he must deal with each alike. Sometimes too a flaw in the work galls him, and he would fain remove it, doing for the poet that which his age denied him; but no, it is not in the bond.

A reading of this paragraph would leave most of us in no doubt that a literal translation is too difficult a task, and would make us turn at once into the easier paths of freedom. This is why Postgate was moved to say that the principle of faithfulness was set up as a merit of true translation 'by general consent, though not by universal practice'. Much that has been written in support of freedom in translation gives just this impression: the translator has shirked the labour of making a close approach to the original words and phrases, and lacks the discipline of self-denial described by Rossetti; whereupon he seeks to discover or to invent a 'principle' to which he can appeal, justifying his own actions and salving his own conscience.

In consequence we are told, often enough, that it is entirely legitimate to include in a translation any idiomatic expression that the original may seem to suggest, or that the first requisite of an English translation is that it shall be English, or that a translation should be able to pass itself off as an original and show all the freshness of original composition. These instructions all add up to a general implication that a translation must be such as may be read with ease and pleasure, coupled with the suggestion that if it is not easy and pleasant it will never be read and might as well never have been made.

The risks lie in the extent of the latitude which the translator permits himself. The limit is found, perhaps, in the casual words of our linguistic friends when we appeal to one of them for help with an almost illegible postcard just received from a foreign correspondent. Amused, they scan the document with an air of superior wisdom, and say 'I can't make it out, exactly, but roughly speaking what it means is ... ' Many must surely have shared this experience, which I have met in my own Common Room, and they will agree that the only thing to do is to examine the card with a magnifying glass and decipher it word by word with a dictionary. Our friend's free translation is too often quite valueless.

A more careful discussion of the characteristics of a translation which is both free and acceptable will bring to light three important points. First, the too brief and dogmatic statement that a translation must read like an original may be supported by a show of reason. The original reads like an original: hence a translation of it should do so too. Common sense suggests that this is so; and the logical development of the notion is that from the translation alone the reader should not be able to determine whether it had been translated from French or Greek, from Arabic or Russian. Whether this is important or not seems to depend solely on the reader and on his reasons for using the translation. To this point we shall return.

Secondly, while there is admittedly a distinction between the original author and his translator, who must constantly remember his debt to the former, a translation is equally the result of original thought and considerable work by the translator. The author has an equivalent debt to his translator, who is in an undeniable degree the proprietor of the translation as such. This proprietorship may be assumed to permit, without further questioning, the introduction of departures from the precise phrasing of the original; and the only doubt remaining is the extent of the departure. This doubt is resolved not by the wishes of the translator, but by the nature of his language. The latitude may be sufficient to make of the translation an example of the translator's language correct in idiom, expression and structure, but it should not be more than this.

Thirdly, there is the fact that, unlike the author, the translator is often one of a number, perhaps a large number, of writers who have preceded him at his task, and a translator of Goethe or Maupassant works with the knowledge that he is the latest of a series of writers who in the past have tried to find the best solutions to the many problems that now face him. This raises a question of some delicacy. If he has conceived a phrase which, he believes, exactly expresses the author's meaning, and if he then finds that one or more of his predecessors have used it already, what should he do? Authority has spoken, not for the first time, with divided opinions. There have been those who have said that a translation, when once made, must not be improved by comparison with its forerunners; and those who have gone further and asserted that such a comparison must be made for the purpose of removing any 'fortuitous coincidences'. This, if strictly applied, is nonsense. Virgil wrote, at the beginning of the Second Aeneid, *'Conticuere omnes'*, which one has translated 'All were hushed' and another as 'All were silent'. What can a new translator suggest? 'They all held their tongues.'

A more acceptable point of view, put forward by Professor Postgate, gives a diametrically opposite opinion. If a translator who has done his best finds that some of his phrases have been used by others before him, he should in no way feel obliged to alter them. On the contrary, he has 'one more reason for their retention'.

54

A translation may include any of the idiomatic expressions that are peculiar to its language and which the translator sees fit to adopt; but it need not, because of this, possess the style which every reader may expect. Style is the essential characteristic of every piece of writing, the outcome of the writer's personality and his emotions at the moment, and no single paragraph can be put together without revealing in some degree the nature of its author. What is true of the author is true also of the translator. The author's style, natural or adopted, determines his choice of a word, and, as has been seen, the translator is often compelled to make a choice between alternatives. The choice he makes cannot but be influenced by his own personality, cannot but reflect, though dimly, his own style. What does the reader expect; what does the critic demand?

One of the reasons for a preference for a literal translation is that it ought to come nearer to the style of the original. It ought to be more accurate; and any copy, whether of a picture or a poem, is likely to be judged by its accuracy. Yet the fact is that in making an attempt to reproduce the effect of the original, too literal a rendering is a mistake, and even the construction of the author's sentences may need alteration in order to transfer their effects to another tongue. As Dr E. V. Rieu says, in introducing his translation of the *Odyssey*, 'In Homer, as in all great writers, matter and manner are inseparably blended ... and if we put Homer straight into English words neither meaning nor manner survives.'

This is the inescapable fact, which advocates of precise, accurate and literal translation cannot gainsay. The ideal that a translator may set before himself has been so admirably described by Ritchie and Moore* that their words must be quoted:

* R. L. G. Ritchie and J. M. Moore, *Translation from French* (C.U.P., 1918).

Suppose that we have succeeded in writing a faithful translation of a characteristic page of Ruskin, and that we submit it for criticism to two well-educated French friends, one of whom has but little acquaintance with English, while the other has an intimate knowledge of our language. If the first were to say 'A fine description! Who is the author?' and the second 'Surely that is Ruskin, though I do not remember the passage,' then we might be confident that in respect of style our translation did not fall too far short of our ideal. We should have written French that was French, while it still kept the flavour of the original.

Here is a striking paragraph. One may feel that the situation envisaged is likely to occur but seldom, and yet as a touchstone of success it is invaluable.

Style is influenced not only by the personality of the writer but also by the period of history in which he lives; and translation includes the bridging of time as well as the bridging of space. Chaucer is usually said to have written English, yet many a reader of *The Canterbury Tales* finds them to be difficult to understand, and is glad to read them in a 'translation' or a version in contemporary English. Later than Chaucer, Archbishop Cranmer wrote in the Book of Common Prayer some of the loveliest English in existence, and yet there are clergymen today who think it desirable to change his words, and to read to their congregations such improvements as 'truly and impartially administer justice', lest our magistrates be thought to be administering an 'indifferent' system of law.

With regard to translation in general, the problem may be put thus. Cervantes published *Don Quixote* in 1605; should that story be translated into contemporary English, such as he would have used at that time had he been an Englishman, or into the English of today? There can be, as a rule, very little doubt as to the answer, for in most cases a reader is justified in expecting to find the kind of English that he is accustomed to use. If a function of translation is to produce in the minds of its readers the same emotions as those produced by the original in the minds of its readers, the answer is clear. Yet there is need to notice in passing the possibility of exceptions whenever the original author is read more for his manner than his matter. We may read the speeches of Cicero, for example, chiefly that we may have an opportunity to appreciate his eloquence. Of recent years the most eloquent speaker of English has been Sir Winston Churchill, and Churchill's style was not Cicero's style. Should a speech by Cicero be so translated as to sound as if it had been delivered by Churchill? No.

We return to the statement made above that the existence of so wide a divergence of opinions among the experts is in itself a phenomenon that calls for explanation.

Part of the explanation is no doubt to be found in the normal variability of the human mind, and this alone is enough to account for a preference by some readers for a literal translation and a preference by others for a free one; for a preference by some for continual reminders that they are reading a translation, and a preference by others for no such thing. But this is not enough to account for the whole of the diversity.

The most probable reason is neglect by the critic of the reader's point of view. Readers of translations do not differ only in their personal preferences, they differ also, and most significantly, in the reasons for which they are reading a translation at all. The primitive function of translation, let it be repeated, is the utilitarian one of overcoming ignorance of the language of the original; but many translations are read by those who know the original language quite as well as does the translator, and who, when they see fit to criticize, cannot rid their minds of this fact. They seem to forget that to the reader who is completely ignorant of the original language, and likely to remain so, their criticisms may seem to be quite pointless, and that such a reader may have found the translation to be pleasing and satisfying. He may even be led to study the original language.

For whom, then, are translations intended? At least four groups can be distinguished.

The first is the reader who knows nothing at all of the original language; who reads either from curiosity or from a genuine interest in a literature of which he will never be able to read one sentence in its original form. The second is the student, who is learning the language of the original, and does so in part by reading its literature with the help of a translation. The third is the reader who knew the language in the past, but who, because of other duties and occupations, has now forgotten almost the whole of his early knowledge. The fourth is the scholar who knows it still.

These four types of readers are obviously using translations for recognizably different purposes, and it must follow from this that, since different purposes are usually achieved by different methods and with the help of different tools, the same translation cannot be equally suited to them all. In other words, this concept of reader-analysis will demonstrate that each form of translation has its own function, which it adequately fulfils when used by the type of reader for whom it was intended.

Let this be amplified. One can so easily imagine the words that form themselves on the lips of readers as they pick up a new volume in translation. The first says to himself, 'What is this book about? Why do I hear other people mention it so often? What of interest has the writer got to say?' The second says, 'This will help me more quickly to understand what the writer had to say about his subject; by quicker reading I shall get a better grasp of his ideas.' The third says, 'Only to think that once, and not so long ago, I was able to read this book properly for myself. How the translation brings it all back: those were the days!' And the fourth says, 'Let me see what poor old So-and-so has made of this. I love it myself; I hope he has not ruined its beauty.'

To these four kinds of readers our four alternative kinds of translations fit themselves naturally and completely.

The ignoramus is happy with the free translation; it satisfies his curiosity, and he reads it easily without the pains of thought. The student is best helped by the most literal translation that can be made in readable English: it helps him to grasp the implications of the different constructions of the language he is studying, and points out the correct usage of the more unfamiliar words. The third prefers the translation that sounds like a translation; it brings back more keenly the memories of his early scholarship and gives him a subconscious impression that he is almost reading the original language. And the fourth, who knows both the matter and style of the original, may find pleasure in occasional touches of scholarship or may, perhaps, enjoy making comments that are more caustic and critical.

Readers of all these kinds abound. Anyone who, like the present writer, has served for nearly twenty years on a Public Library Committee, knows that the 'average borrower' is a fictitious personage who is not to be found among the rate-payers of his district; and that of any work of great reputation every translation that is put on the library shelves will have its own share of admirers. Further than this, many a borrower may consult more than one translation. Two translations are four times as good as one, and in the broad span of literary adventure there is a welcome place for them all.

V

Translating the classics

It is useless to read Greek in translations: translators can but offer us a
vague equivalent.

VIRGINIA WOOLF

More than half of all that has been written on the subject of
translation has been concerned with the classical languages
and the difficulties that are found in reading them. Sometimes
it seems to be assumed that the word translation means the
rendering of Latin and Greek into English. The reason for
this is the importance of these languages in the education of
those who subsequently follow a literary life, but there is no
problem inherent in the translation of Latin or Greek that
cannot be paralleled in the translation of any other language,
as long as the act of translation is regarded as a linguistic
manoeuvre and no more.

But the translation of Greek must be more than linguistic
practice, because Greek is one of the supreme literary
languages of the world; there is that about Greek that is
possessed by no other language. What is the secret of the
ascendancy of Greek in the minds of scholars?

Even though it is true, it is not very helpful to say that it
has charm, for charm itself is an elusive quality and one
which Greek shares with both French and Russian. It is more
than usually difficult to define when it is the charm of a
language that rises above its topic and is appreciated by its
readers, independently of its subject matter. Mrs Virginia
Woolf expresses it by saying that 'it is the language that
holds us most in bondage' for it is harmonious, musical,
expressive, compact.

Its harmony is in part the result of an avoidance of all discords. The consonants fall short, in use, of the preponderance that the alphabet appears to give them, and especially they are absent from the final position in a word. Greek words that end in consonants almost always end in γ or ρ or ς, and very seldom in any other. The lightness which this alone imparts to a Greek sentence is sustained and amplified by the frequency of the brighter vowels α, ε, and ο, and the rarity of the hard, anaemic ι and υ.

The rhythm of a sentence and of a paragraph is almost wholly the result of the interplay and variation of its vowels, and in Greek such variation is assured by the abundance of diphthongs. These not only affect the exact meaning; they change the intensities of accentuation and give a varied modulation to the succession of sentences of which any passage must be composed.

In consequence the words of the Greek language, separately and by themselves, have a music that is scarcely to be heard in the words of other languages. Mrs Woolf instances θάλασσα, θάνατος ἄνθος, ἄστηρ and σελήνη, and indeed her selection would be difficult to surpass in Latin or French, Italian or Spanish. When, at the famous climax of the march of Xenophon's Ten Thousand, the weary soldiers saw the waters of the Black Sea, they ran and shouted '*Thalassa, thalassa!*' The words have passed into history, and in 1908 when Professor David's party in the Antarctic struggled across the Drygalski Ice Barrier and saw the Ross Sea, they too shouted '*Thalassa!*' The words themselves are satisfying, expressive, exultant. In different circumstances other men might have shouted '*La mer!*' or '*Die See!*'; but would such syllables have embedded themselves in the memories of readers for generations to come; would they have been worth the shouting; or, if shouted, worth the recording?

However, men do not use language in order to emit

pleasurable sounds, but to give audible expression to their thoughts, and Greek excels in its ability to respond to the finest shades of implication and emphasis. It can do this because its full declensions and conjugations provide a completeness of inflections to be found nowhere else*; and, as if this were not enough, the use of particles, bewildering as they may be to students, add a further refinement to the language. There is small wonder that Greek has been described as 'the noblest form of human speech' or as a language 'without a peer for the expression of human thought'.

For many generations past, scholars have come to admire the Greek tongue and have wished to pass on their admiration to their students. Until the beginning of the present century, some knowledge of Greek was a normal possession of every educated man. Readers will recall a short conversation in *Ravenshoe*:

> ... 'I am not a gentleman; I am a gamekeeper's son.' 'I suppose you can read Greek, now, can't you?' said the coachman. Charles was obliged to confess that he could. 'Of course,' said the coachman; 'all gamekeepers' sons is forced to learn Greek, in order that they may slang the poachers in an unknown tongue.'

Today a knowledge of Greek is evidence only of an education of a particular kind, and is an accomplishment that is becoming annually rarer. And yet, while there is an increase in the proportion of British citizens who can lead useful and even important lives without regretting their ignorance of Greek, there are also many who are anxious to know something, at least, of the literature of ancient Greece, and for whom translations are invaluable. They provide the best means of making contact with the Greek spirit, a spirit that has influenced almost every literature in the world.

* Except, possibly, in Finnish. See Note 1.

These preliminary considerations help us to understand the general and conspicuous division of all translators into two groups, described by Higham and Bourne as 'Hellenizers' and 'Modernizers'. Perhaps they are only a subdivision of a special case of the familiar categories of the faithful and the free, and certainly Higham and Bourne were writing only about Greek verse; but even so they demand attention.

The aim of the Hellenizer is to bring his translation, and its reader, as near as possible to the original Greek, preserving always its literal sense, and including, as far as may be, its characteristic idioms. The Modernizer takes the contrary view and attempts to produce an English equivalent for the Greek, something analogous to it, perhaps, but on the whole Britannic rather than Hellenic. A simple example will illustrate the difference; it is taken from the parable of the sower. The Greek of St Luke viii, 8, reads:

καὶ ἕτερον ἔπεσεν ἔπι τὴν γῆν τὴν ἀγαθήν

for which the Authorized Version has 'And others fell on good ground'. This is a Modernizer's translation, giving good, plain English. A Hellenizer would feel that the characteristic way in which the adjective ἀγαθήν followed the noun γῆν had been neglected and its implication lost. St Luke had not written ἔπι τὴν ἀγαθήν γῆν, he had written words that laid a slightly different emphasis on the adjective – 'on ground which was good', or something like this. A Hellenizer would try to express the distinction in this and in other comparable cases. Whether he would succeed is another matter.

As usual, there is plenty of support for both sides of the question. Robert Browning, for example, explains in the Preface to his translation of the *Agamemnon* that if he had had need of the services of a translator he would have wanted him to be 'literal at every cost save that of absolute violence to our language'. He supports his opinion by adding that for 'so immensely famous' an original he would excuse even a clumsy attempt to give him 'the very turn of each phrase in as Greek a fashion as English will bear'.

While Browning appears to have considered the fame of the original as a deciding factor, Robert Bridges believed that the style of the writer is of importance to the reader of a translation. It is misleading, he says, to produce a translation of Homer which reminds the reader of Milton or Tennyson or Swinburne, because Homer does not do this: a translation of Homer should read so that it suggests Homer, and no one else.

Both these reasonings seem to be sound enough, but so also do the arguments from the opposite point of view. There is no justification, it is said, for trying to force English into a Grecian, or any other, mould, because the touches of Greek idiom will not be detected or appreciated by Greekless readers. The line of Hymn 181, 'We know Thee, who Thou art,' will not, to such readers, recall a Greek construction; it will only sound like curious English. Both Edward Fitzgerald and Samuel Butler are concerned that the translation must at any cost be easily readable; the former asserts a preference for a live sparrow rather than a stuffed eagle; and the latter says, quite simply, that a construe, however good it may be, is not a translation.

These contrasting opinions find more emphatic expression in the translation of Homer than of any other writer, and no doubt this must inevitably be so. Homer wrote Greek that, in the eyes of scholars ever since, has been surpassed by no other writer, and because of this his reputation stands high above all others. In consequence translators are expected to give us both the matter of Homer's famous poems and also the manner of Homer's writing.

Difficult as this may be, there has never been a lack of

scholars who were willing to make the attempt; to try to match their English to Homer's Greek. Whatever their successes, they have always found readers ready to meet them with less sympathy than criticism. 'Every generation,' says Dr F. A. Wright, 'sees fresh corpses added to the pile round Homer and Sappho and Horace.' He suggests that there must be some fascination about these three, luring translators to a siren shore, where they leave their bones whitening in the sand. There is so much truth in this that one is inclined to believe the late Provost of King's almost literally when he said* that 'the only purpose of education is to enable one to read Homer in the original Greek'.

The student of translation is fortunate when he comes to consider the problems of Homer, for he may read in Matthew Arnold's *Essays Literary and Critical* his well-known essay *On Translating Homer*. This essay was mentioned in Chapter III. It was provoked by a translation made by F. W. Newman, Professor of Latin at University College, London, who was a thorough-going Hellenist. In his own words, he tried 'to retain every peculiarity of the original so far as he is able, with the greater care, the more foreign it may happen to be'. Thus he was one of those who wished their readers never to forget that the translation they are reading is an imitation.

Arnold was vehemently opposed to this. His interpretation of faithfulness in translation was given a characteristic and unusual touchstone, namely, that the translation shall affect a scholar who knows Greek and who also appreciates poetry, with the same sensations as does the original. We were told that if this was to be done the translator must be thoroughly imbued with the four chief qualities of Homer, his rapidity, his plain directness, first in words and secondly in ideas, and his nobleness of thought. Undoubtedly all this is easier to advise than to achieve.

* Sir John T. Sheppard, at Malvern College Speech Day, June 1949.

Another problem that Homer sets to the translator is that of metre. The Homeric hexameter has been described by Wright as 'miraculous in lightness and strength', while an English hexameter is regarded as a 'monstrosity'. This is a severe condemnation of a metre which has to its credit such lines as 'This is the forest primaeval, the murmuring pines and the hemlock', or 'Blossom and blossom and promise of blossom, but never a fruit', and is not the view that was taken by Arnold. He discussed, for possible use in translating epic poetry, the alternatives of heroic couplets, blank verse, and hexameters; and concluded with very strong support for the last of these. Apparently one of his favourite passages in the *Iliad* is the conclusion of the Eighth Book, for he uses this more than once to illustrate his opinions. His own prose translation of the last lines was:

> There were kindled a thousand fires in the plain; and by each one there sat fifty men in the light of the blazing fire. And the horses, munching white barley and rye, and standing by the chariots, waited for the bright-throned morning.

To compare this, or the original Greek, with Alexander Pope's heroic couplets is interesting:

> A thousand piles the dusky horrors gild,
> And shoot a shady lustre o'er the field.
> Full fifty guards each flaming pile attend
> Whose umbered arms, by fits, thick flashes send;
> Loud neigh the coursers o'er their heaps of corn,
> And ardent warriors wait the rising morn.

The above passage is as good as any for justifying the comment made on Pope's verse that he 'could not call it Homer'. Lord Tennyson's blank verse is:

66

So many a fire between the ships and stream
Of Xanthus blazed before the towers of Troy,
A thousand on the plain; and close by each
Sat fifty in the blaze of burning fire;
And eating hoary grain and pulse the steeds
Fixt by their cars, waited the golden dawn.

Matthew Arnold justified his faith in the English hexameter
thus:

In the plain there were kindled a thousand fires; by each
one
There sat fifty men in the ruddy light of the fire;
By their chariots stood the steeds, and champed the
white barley
While their masters sat by the fire and waited for morning.

In comparison with the translating of Homer, the translation of the drama of Greece demands little space. If ever
there were a phase of translation in which the principle of
the modernizer was incontestably to be preferred, it is in the
rendering of a Greek play. The reason is not far to seek.
With the somewhat rare exceptions of occasional passages,
Greek drama never reached the supreme perfection of
Homer, and regrettably but undoubtedly true is the fact that
a non-Grecian may read a rather too literal translation of a
Greek play and be moved to laugh at it where no laughter
was intended. Not for such unappreciative amusement does
a translator undertake to make a rendering of *The Frogs* or
Oedipus Rex. He can avoid this and preserve a claim to
faithfulness by acceptable modernization.

An essential and characteristic feature of both Greek prose
and Latin prose is the influence on its development of the
practice of oratory. The young Athenian strove to acquire
competence in public speaking and agility in debate. The

practice of speaking aloud acquired the distinction of an art with which all educated men were expected to be familiar. The same ideals were held by the young Roman, and so lead us to consider the Latin language.

Gradually the reputation of Athens as a seat of learning faded while that of Rome grew. Scholars from a wide area converged on Rome, and Sulla brought with him a Greek library from Athens. Roman students acquired without question the ability to read and speak Greek, and in the great library planned by Caesar and, in the event, founded by Augustus, there were two chief departments, Latin and Greek.

Thus the practice of oratory developed in Rome even as once it had flourished in Athens. The characteristics of the style that was best suited to rhetoric were sought, and were defined as *elegantia*, *compositio* and *dignitas*. The first of these covered clearness of expression derived from a correct choice of words, the second involved the best arrangement of the words chosen, while the third was concerned with correctness of sentiment. This admiration for rhetoric had a greater influence than any other single factor on the evolution of the ultimate character of the language which was used by Cicero and Caesar. It was different from Greek, and it would be difficult to deny that in many respects it was inferior. With the precision of its grammar, its relatively few monosyllables, restricted vowel sounds and uniformity of accent, it could not show the harmony or claim the subtlety of Greek. It had not the compound words so characteristic of Greek; its words were sharper. These qualities gave it a strength which showed itself in several ways. Those who have praised Greek most extravagantly have also said of Latin that it had a precision and force not easily to be found elsewhere. 'The directness of a Latin sentence marks it as the speech of men who knew exactly what they wanted to say, and said it with all the force at their command.' Such a quality is admirable in any language, and it gave Latin a strength that resulted in its survival.

Greek of the highest quality was written only for a relatively short time; the language of Demosthenes is so far removed from that of Epicurus and Polybius that evidence of decay is irrefutable. Latin did not suffer and has not suffered the same deterioration, but developed into the rich prose of Livy and, through the poetry of Catullus, to that of Ovid, Horace and Virgil. So great was the practical value of Latin that it continued in use as a literary language until medieval times, a language well able to meet all the demands made upon it.

For example, a language of such precision was the ideal one in which the law could be stated; it was used until quite recently by biologists for the writing of their accurate and succinct diagnoses of plants and animals; and further proof of its versatility comes from its worldwide use in prayer. In his *Autobiography*, the Reverend J. O. Hannay finds reason to complain of the mediocrity of the prayers composed by bishops for special occasions. He explains this by saying that 'no good collect can be written originally in any language except Latin'; and he suggests that bishops who have not forgotten how to do so should compose prayers in Latin and then have them translated.

Canon Hannay's praise for the language in which the Creator may be fitly addressed can be seen to be justified, and something of the nature of Latin prose can surely be appreciated, even by those whose knowledge of the language is vestigial, by a reading of the following. The familiar words of the English version reach an equally high standard, which is exactly Canon Hannay's thesis;

Tenebras nostras illumina, quaesumus, o Domine, et nos per immensam misericordiam tuam ab omnibus hujusce noctis insidiis atque periculis immunes praesta, propter caritatem filii sui unigeniti, Jesu Christi, Servatoris nostri.

Inevitably, all Latin prose does not read like this, or evoke the same kind of English equivalent. In the translation, so familiar to many of us, of the writings of Caesar, the parallelism to the translation of Xenophon is evident. Both show us an unusual combination of the man of action and the man of letters, both were men who had seen and done things beyond the run of ordinary citizens, and both were able to tell those ordinary citizens about the things that they had done. Both, moreover, were fortunate in their choice of subject. The *Anabasis*, or *The Retreat of the Ten Thousand*, and *De Bello Gallico*, or *The Gallic War*, were concerned with matters which exactly suited them both, and as a result there is often less difficulty than usual in transfusing the spirit of their words into the words of another language.

Searching for an example, we alight on Caesar's tribute to the unnamed standard-bearer of the Tenth Legion, whose courage was equal to the challenge of a critical moment during the first landing of the Romans in Britain:

Atque nostris militibus cunctantibus, maxime propter altitudinem maris, qui decimae legonis aquilam ferebat, contestatus deos, ut ea res legioni feliciter eveniret, 'Desilite,' inquit, 'milites, nisi vultis aquilam hostibus prodere: ego certe meum rei publicae atque imperatori officium praestitero.' Hoc cum voce magna dixisset, se ex navi proiecit atque in hostes aquilam ferre coepit. Tum nostri cohortati inter se, ne tantum dedecus admitteretur, universi ex navi desiluerunt.

Then, as our men were hanging back, chiefly because the water was so deep, the eagle-bearer of the Tenth Legion, with a prayer to the gods to favour the legion because of his action, cried, 'Leap, men, unless you wish to betray the Eagle to the foe! It shall be said that I at least did my duty to my fatherland and to my commander.' When he had said this with a loud voice, he leapt from his ship and began to carry the Eagle towards the enemy; so that our men encouraged each other not to allow such disgrace, and with one accord jumped down from their vessels.*

Lest the translation of Latin should be thought to be 'easy' this chapter may be concluded with the treatment of Latin verse. Of the three Latin poets mentioned above, Ovid, Virgil and Horace, the last is given the greater part of a chapter to himself, and Virgil is chosen instead of Ovid for three reasons. First, because he was, in the words of Tennyson,

> Wielder of the noblest measure
> Ever moulded by the lips of man,

which, by itself, entitles him to some claim to priority; secondly, because to most readers his poetry and in particular the *Aeneid* is more familiar than any other Latin verse, and thirdly, because some readers will have had the opportunity of hearing for themselves the story of Aeneas, translated and broadcast by C. Day Lewis.

In this the translator faced all the problems which poetry always presents, and which are mentioned in Chapter VI. Mr Day Lewis carries us through them with an enviable sureness of touch. Granted, he says, in effect, that to discover what Virgil meant is seldom difficult, to reproduce the way in which he said it is all but impossible. To shirk this impossibility and to give the story of the *Aeneid* in prose, our natural medium for narrative, he dismisses as being

* See Note 2.

unworthy of an epic; and he concludes his introduction by telling us that if the translator is to catch the tone and spirit of his author there must be a kind of spiritual sympathy between the two. This affinity he aptly describes as the translator's talisman; but he can give us no hint as to its discovery, save to say that one can find it only by luck.

Here is a suggestion, and more, of a new conception in translation at its highest level. In addition to familiarity with the language of the original, in addition to ability in writing English, and in addition to knowledge of the subject matter, there is to be sought a psychical affinity between author and translator. This is, indeed, a fascinating hypothesis, worth further exploration, implying, as it does, that for the translation of a given work Mr X may be a better choice than Mr Y, not because of his literary ability nor because of his scholarship, but chiefly because of his personality.

The reader may enjoy applying these principles to the scene in which Laocoon warns his fellow Trojans against the possible dangers of the Wooden Horse. He came, it will be remembered, running from the citadel,

> *magna comitante caterva*
> girt with a throng of Ilium's sons (Conington)
> hundreds straggling behind him   (Day Lewis)

and crying:

> *et procul; 'o miseri, quae tanta insania, cives?*
> *creditis avectos hostes? aut illa putatis*
> *dona carere dolis Danaum? sic notus Ulixes?*
> *aut hoc inclusi ligno occultantur Achivi,*
> *aut haec in nostros fabricata est machina mures*
> *inspectura domos venturaque desuper urbi;*
> *aut aliquis latet error; equo ne credite, Teucri,*
> *quiquid id est, timeo Danaos et dona ferrentes.'*

In a more or less literal construe this reads:

(He cried) from afar, 'O wretched citizens, what is this great madness? Do you think that the enemy has gone? Do you think that any present from the Greeks is without guile? Is that your opinion of Ulysses? Either Greeks are hidden, shut up in this wooded thing, or it is a machine built (to fight) against our walls, to overlook our houses and o'ertop the city; or else some trick is hidden: trust not the horse, Trojans, whatever it is I fear the Greeks, even when they bring gifts.'

The rhyming version of Connington (1861) runs:

'Wretched countrymen,' he cries,
'What monstrous madness blinds your eyes?
  Think you your enemies removed?
  Come presents without wrong
From Danaans? have you thus approved
  Ulysses, known so long?
Perchance — who knows? — the bulk we see
  Conceals a Grecian enemy,
Or 'tis a pile to o'erlook the town,
And pour from high invaders down,
Or fraud lurks somewhere to destroy:
Mistrust, mistrust it, men of Troy!
Whate'er it be, a Greek I fear,
Though presents in his hand he bear.'

Thirdly, Mr Day Lewis* has given us:

'Citizens, are you all stark mad?
Do you really believe our foes are gone? Do you imagine
Any Greek gift is guileless? Is that your idea of Ulysses?
This thing of wood conceals Greek soldiers, or else it is

* C. Day Lewis, *The Aeneid of Virgil* (Hogarth Press, 1952).

A mechanism designed against our walls – to pry into
Our houses and to bear down on the city; sure, some trick
Is there. No, you must never feel safe with the horse,
   Trojans,
Whatever it is, I distrust the Greeks, even when they are
   generous.'

This short passage from the *Aeneid* was not introduced only
to compare the translation of Latin prose with the translation
of Latin verse, but also to show how different translators
have rendered the same original. Another aspect of the same
phenomenon is the reason which causes a particular translator to be drawn to the translation of a particular book or
poem and to give it much time and thought.

I have written very little about Greek drama, and nothing
about the historians Herodotus and Thucydides, but this
chapter could not be closed without a reference to and
acknowledgment of the genius of Professor Gilbert Murray,
as shown in his translations of Greek plays. So, too, one
should recall the undoubted triumph of Professor H. S.
Butcher and Dr Andrew Lang, in their prose versions of the
Odyssey and the *Iliad*. But the translators of classical Latin
and Greek are so many that it would be absurd, in a small
book, to embark on an evaluation of them all; it were wiser
to record the gratitude of their countless untutored readers,
pausing to consider how much would have been lost if their
efforts had not been preserved for us to study and to enjoy.

VI

The translation of poetry

All translation seems to me to be simply an attempt to solve an insoluble problem.

HUMBOLDT

The translation of poetry and, with it, the translation of verse, form a distinct, isolated, and extremely important section of the art with which this book is concerned. It is almost the only aspect of translation in which a high proportion of the experts show agreement among themselves; but even so they agree only in the opinion that adequate translation of a poem is impossible. They disagree in the usual way about the best methods by which the impossible may be attempted, as well as in their criticisms and appraisals of the attempts that have been made.

Let the matter of impossibility be discussed first.

What is poetry? It is 'the art of employing words in such a manner as to produce an illusion on the senses: the art of doing by means of words what the painter does by means of colours.' Poetry, then, produces an illusion; it acquires memorableness by certain features which can be more easily recognized than reproduced at will. There is rhythm, metrical rhythm; there is emotion, sensuous emotion; there is an increased use of figures of speech and a degree of disregard for conventional word-order; there is imagination, and, above all, there is an ability to see features in an object or a situation which another, not a poet, might miss.

All this is true, but what strikes the reader as being equally true is that none of it is the prerogative of any one language. The power to write with emotion, rhythm and percipience

75

is, and always has been, possessed by men of all nations. Cannot an Englishman, a German and a Greek show this power in the same way in the face of the same inspiration? The answer, apparently, is that they cannot.

This brings us face to face with the so-called impossibility of translation, an impossibility of which Anatole France is reported to have said: 'Precisely, my friend; recognition of that truth is a necessary preliminary to success in the art,' an oxymoron which provokes the question: 'What, then, is meant by the facile statement that perfect translation is impossible?' It can mean only that in the act of translation something that the author has to offer to the reader is lost, and that the loss mars the theoretical perfection of the translation.

Of course this presupposes that in the original there was something the loss of which would be noticeable. And there may not have been:

> *'Baa, baa, mouton noir,*
> *Avez-vous de la laine?'*
> *'Oui, monsieur, oui, monsieur,*
> *Trois poches pleines.*
> *Une pour le maître et*
> *Une pour la demoiselle*
> *Et une pour le petit garçon*
> *Qui vit dans notre ruelle.'*

These lines were committed to memory by the present writer more than half a century ago, and now they are of some use as an example of translation which is perfect because the original had no scholarship, no subtlety, nor even any sense.

To object that this example is irrelevant because its theme is infantile is to fail to appreciate the fact that the elementary must contain the fundamentals and must illustrate the same principles as does the advanced. A second example will

therefore be given, one which equally demonstrates the
width of the gulf between a piece of verse and its translation,
and which is also taken from the nursery. The gulf here is one
of sound, not of verbal content.

Many years ago small children in France derived pleasure
from the jingle:

> *Quand un gendarme rit*
> *Dans la gendarmerie*
> *Tous les gendarmes rient*
> *Dans la gendarmerie.*

Perhaps they still do so: I do not know, but I am sure that no
English child would be likely to remember or to repeat:
'When a policeman laughs in the police station, all the
policemen laugh in the police station.'

These examples are not ludicrous: they give point to the
idea that losses in translation occur only when the original
words contain something more than their plain meanings.
This something more may be found in a harmony between
sense and sound, or in a subtle alliteration, or literary device.
In the absence of these a verse may contain a studied simplicity which may be more effective than any decoration,
and which may be found to have been expressed with no loss
of effectiveness when a translation has been made:

> A little sleep, a little slumber,
>   A little folding of the hands to sleep;
> So shall thy poverty come as a robber
>   And thy want, as an armed man.
>
>   or
>
> *Un peu de sommeil, un peu d'assoupissement,*
>   *Un peu croiser les mains pour dormir;*
> *Et la pauvreté te surprendra comme un voleur*
>   *Et la disette, comme un homme en armes.*

77

or

Schlafe noch ein wenig, schlummere ein wenig,
Schlage die Hände in einander dass du schläfest;
So wird dich die Armuth übereilen wie ein Fussgänger,
Und der Mangel, wie ein gewaffneter Mann.

(Proverbs, vi, 10–11)

None of these translations has lost anything that the original is found to express and there is no doubt about the quality of all.

All poetry, however, is not written with such simplicity as this, and no great power of penetration is needed to see that the very developments and complications which distinguish poetry from prose are the characteristics which cannot be translated. In writing poetry the poet chooses his words with more attention to their sounds than is customary or necessary in the writing of prose, and in translating the sound is more often than not changed considerably. 'Horse and hound' is not the same sound as *le cheval et le chien* or as *equus et canis*: 'hill and dale' is not the same as *Hügel und Tal* or *cuesta y valle*; and no power or system exists which will make the words in one language produce the aural effect they possess in another.

When Virgil wrote

Quadrupedante putrem sonitu quatit ungula campum

he wrote a line which has ever since been famous because its rhythm and its accents suggest the thudding of the hooves of a galloping horse, but no translator can preserve and reproduce this. All that can be done for the reader who knows no Latin is to explain to him the meaning of each word separately, so that he may be able to answer the first of the questions posed in Chapter II, What does he say?, and then to leave the music of the verse

78

to seep into his mind by the familiarity that comes with repetition.

If this construing can be done for one line it can presumably be done for more than one. The result, when committed to paper, is no more than an approach to a prose translation of the poem, and so leads us to the last pair of alternatives listed in Chapter IV:

11. A translation of verse should be in prose.
12. A translation of verse should be in verse.

This divided opinion must here be discussed.

One of the most telling paragraphs in Professor Postgate's *Translation and Translations* states as a cardinal principle the rule that prose should be translated by prose and verse by verse; and adds that whereas no one doubts the first statement, many are prepared to argue about the second. For example, Matthew Arnold expressed the opinion that a prose translation of poetry may still be highly poetical, but Carlyle, Leigh Hunt and Archbishop Whately agreed that poetry is incomplete without the aesthetic effects of metre. Lord Woodhouselee said that a prose translation of a lyric is the most absurd of all such ventures and that none but a poet should translate a poem; whereas Hilaire Belloc stated dogmatically that 'translation of verse is nearly always better rendered in prose'.

Remembering Postgate's remorseless logic, prose into prose, verse into verse, we shall be well advised first to consider the arguments in favour of verse translation. These arguments and opinions are all concentrated in an often quoted sentence from Sir John Denham's Preface to the Second Book of the *Aeneid*: 'The business is not alone to translate language into language, but poesie into poesie, and poesie is of so subtle a spirit that in the pouring out of one language into another it will all evaporate, and if a new

79

spirit is added in the transfusion there will remain nothing but a *caput mortuum*.' We should try to discover the steps that led to this summary.

One of these is no doubt the fact that verse translation more closely resembles the form of the original. A verse translation at least gives the opportunity to indulge in figures of speech and to adopt the varied word-order which the original contained, and which some translators wish to preserve wherever possible. In general, the power of verse to stir the emotions is greater than is the power of prose, so that to choose to make a prose translation of a poem is to impose a handicap on the translator and to ask for a sacrifice of a portion of his effect before he has begun. The following example, simple as it is, establishes the truth of these remarks. Catullus wrote:

> *Odi et amo, quare id faciam fortasse requiris,*
> *nescio, sed fieri sentio et excrucior.*

In prose this becomes, 'I hate and I love. Why I do so perhaps you ask: I do not know, but I feel it and I am in agony.' Compare that flabby complaint with the sharp pain of the original and with Mrs Krause's crisp couplet:

> I hate yet love. You ask how this can be.
> I only know its truth and agony

and the comparison shows clearly enough that verse can give the meaning of the original together with something that at least approaches and suggests the manner.

When one is told by such experienced translators as Archer and Lenard that they have found that in verse they could be more exact, more accurate than in prose, the principle of 'verse for verse' may seem to be established beyond doubt.

If this is so, and verse is really the most appropriate setting for the translation of verse, there arises the pertinent question why prose translations should ever have been considered at all by translators, and why in some collections – an example is the famous, the indispensable Loeb Library – the proportion of published prose translations actually exceeds the verse. An answer is soon discovered by anyone who tries to put a few lines of Greek, Latin, or French poetry into English verse. His first step is to make a prose translation, to be quite sure, perhaps, that he knows what he is going to say, and then to reshape his words, converting them into verse. But verse, satisfying verse, does not normally rise to the lips or flow from the pen unbidden; and the translator finds himself devoting thought and sacrificing time in the effort to find the right words and so secure the best result. Here is a practical demonstration that a verse translation demands more effort and more skill than a prose one. Should one be asked how much more, the answers are : first, that different skills cannot be compared; secondly, that Sir George Young wrote of his translation of Sophocles that 'it was undertaken forty years ago for pleasure and has been executed with pain'; and thirdly, that more recently Mr Cyril Connolly has recorded that he once took a week to translate eight lines of Propertius.

Further, though this is a contradiction of an opinion mentioned above, there is general admission that a prose translation can be made to come nearer to the phrasing and construction of the original. Is this what is wanted most?

Doubts and dissents such as these can be attacked only by the method, already introduced in Chapter II, which I have called reader-analysis. Our present discussion is about the translation of poetry; hence the first question to be asked and answered is : Why does anyone read poetry? This is a question that each reader must answer for himself.

I may read a lyric for its sensuous effect, for its acute contrast to normal prose, in which no such effect is to be found.

At the right moment the reading of a short poem has some-times the effect of a rest after a journey, sometimes the effect of a shot of benzedrine. If I read *Paradise Lost* it is not because I wish to know Milton's ideas on Ptolemaic cosmogony, and if Milton had wanted me to do so he would have written a treatise on cosmogony, as Dr H. Jeffreys has done, and not an epic, as he did. Or I may read the ode of Horace that begins *'Integer vitae sclerisque purus'* not because I am interested in the evasive behaviour of Sabine wolves, nor did Horace expect it of me. I read the epic because I am affected by the incomparable majesty of Milton's blank verse; I read the ode because I enjoy its climax in the inimitable music of its last two lines:

> *dulce ridentem Lalagen amabo,*
> *dulce loquentem.*

In a word, the primary purpose of reading poetry is for poetry's sake.

There are other readers, less fortunate, who are compelled to read a poem, long or short, in the cause of education, and at this stage it is generally a matter of indifference to them whether it is great poetry, or poor poetry, or not poetry. There are others again, poets themselves or poets-to-be, who read that haply they may absorb the poet's spirit and learn something of his secret.

This analysis has made our choice clearer. The reader who seeks the music and the majesty that may lie in a pattern of words is the reader who can never be put off with a prose translation, whereas the student wants little else. Writers who have recommended the translation of poetry into prose have done so because they were thinking of one particular function of the translation, to show how the lines may be construed. When the student has learnt this he will be content with the original and will not need a translation in any form.

82

Others, again, are not concerned with obtaining help in studying the language. If they are never going to attempt to read the original, they want a substitute for it; and so the translator, always generous, tries to provide them with something that will satisfy their needs.

At the very start he meets, and must answer, a vital question. English poetry, like French and German, is normally rhymed; Latin and Greek poetry is not. Hence in translating a French or German poem the translator will not hesitate to attempt a rhymed version:

> *Die Luft ist kühl und es dunkelt*
> *Und ruhig fliesst der Rhein,*
> *Der Gipfel des Berges funkelt*
> *Im Abendsonnenschein*

becomes

> Chilly the air and darkling,
>   Soft the Rhine flows,
> The peak of the mountain, sparkling
>   In sunset, glows.

This is, at the same time, the normal English practice and it gives a rendering which is more like the original; but in translating a Greek or Latin poem a rhymed translation will not be like the original, save only in the indirect sense that it is more likely to evoke the same sensations among English readers as were evoked among its readers by the unrhymed original depending on accent and rhythm.

Such arguments in favour of rhyme may be expanded. First, the classical dramas contained both dialogue and chorus, and there is little doubt that the songs should be put into rhyme, for this serves the purpose of suitably distinguishing them from the dialogue. If the latter is also in rhyme this cannot be done so effectively. Further, the different metres used in dialogue and chorus can better be emphasized by the introduction of rhyme than in any other way; and rhyme better than anything else can be made to indicate the arrangement of the original verses in couplets or stanzas.

All these are theoretical arguments which would have great force if all languages had an infinite number of words, and a larger proportion of words of exact equivalence, and were themselves all infinitely pliable. But no two languages are matched like this; and all the theoretical arguments tend to disappear before practical experience, which discovers that rhyme is an infernal nuisance. How is this?

Rhyme imposes a constraint upon a writer, a constraint which bears most heavily on the essential feature of the translator's art, his choice of words. One can scarcely find a rhymed translation of a lyric which does not contain evidence of this, as shown either by the omission of something that the original author wrote, or the inclusion of something that he did not. Mr Oliver Edwards, writing in *The Times* in June 1955, was good enough to confess to a complete modern example of this. Translating a Welsh poem, 'hen Benillion', he wrote the line

And still the crow feeds by the shore

and in discussing his work, admits 'some liberty' with the crow, which in the original was tending its nest 'and won't rhyme in English'.

There, in short space, is the problem of rhyme in translation. Its deficiencies and disadvantages are so many that writers on the subject of translation take them for granted, and have promoted them from the low grading of translational imperfections to the better-sounding status of additions and subtractions. Lord Woodhouselee, for example, devoted the third chapter of his book to the question 'whether it is allowable for a translator to add to or retrench the ideas of the original'. One's instinctive answer to such a proposition is surely an emphatic 'No', nor is this only a natural wish for accuracy. Why should a translator wish to omit anything that his author has written, unless it be from laziness or from a wish to hide his own ignorance of what is meant; and why, still less, should a translator have the impertinence to put into his author's mouth words that he has never spoken? The only possible answer to these questions is that the translator has been forced to do so because he has handicapped himself with the tyranny of rhyme.

By some writers, however, these enormities are concealed or condoned by the establishment of a principle of 'compensation'. If a translator finds himself compelled to omit something, he may be excused if he offers something else in its place, as if he were a merchant who, having promised to deliver a specified weight of some commodity, has failed to do so and must make amends by the gift of an unexpected bonus. When Woodhouselee wrote, the practice was so common as to be taken for granted, and his book includes a section in which he discusses 'the freedom allowed to a poetical translator'. Yet it is, obviously, a practice that involves a risk and is liable to be misused. Modern opinion scarcely condones it. Rhyme has lost much of the inevitability that tradition has given it, with results that cannot easily be exaggerated when the translation of poetry is in question. The contemporary writers of prose-poetry or poetic prose are bound neither to the tyranny of rhyme nor even to the exactitude of stress and accent insisted on by past generations, and they have thus gained for themselves the opportunity of giving in translation both the meaning and the movement, the matter and the manner, of a poem in another language.

With metres less customary in English poetry, such as the elegiacs of the classics, this method often holds the greatest potentialities. It became more widely known when Dr

Robert Bridges used what he described as 'loose Alexandrines' in *The Testament of Beauty*, a poem which not only demonstrated the power of the prose-poem diction but also, regretfully, exposed its tendency to monotony.

The very fact that the translation may be a poem made of English words is in itself of importance, for it warns us not to overstress the so-called impossibility of translation. It is so tempting to admit the popular judgment, and perhaps to use it as an excuse for not doing what may indeed be difficult, but which is therefore more satisfying when or if successfully attempted. It leads us, moreover, to another consideration.

So far we have written solely about translation into English; is it possible that English has characteristics which make it more, or less, suitable for this purpose than other languages?

English has a large vocabulary, more varied and more extensive than that of Latin or French; and often the same kind of idea can be expressed in a simple native word, or in a less simple, derived one: for example, 'healthy', or 'sanitary' (Latin), or 'hygienic' (Greek). But whereas this may ease (or facilitate) the translator's work (or operation) by giving him greater breadth (or latitude) of expression, it makes translating harder by forcing him to make the best possible choice from among the various alternatives. Thus the advantage of a large vocabulary is in practice reduced.

Again, English has no inflexions, so that its words cannot always be rearranged so as to produce by their arrangement a part of the effect that is sought. The order of the words has to fulfil part of the functions of grammar, and if the order is disturbed the sense may be disproportionately affected. 'And all the air a solemn stillness holds' is a pleasant enough line from Gray's 'Elegy', but it contains no clue as to whether 'air' or 'stillness' is subject or object. In the related German language the same line might be

Und all die Luft hält feierliche Stille

and the same ambiguity remains. Such a doubt would not persist in Latin or Greek, and its presence here shows that English cannot claim to be the ideal language for translators.

English is not sufficiently flexible to be cast into such moulds as those found in the classical metres. We may recall Tennyson's deliberate 'experiment':

> When was a harsher sound ever heard, ye Muses, in England?
> When did a frog coarser croak upon our Helicon?

It has more consonants and fewer vowels, a fact which stiffens it; and its monosyllables, admirable as they are in the right setting, do not easily adapt themselves to a strange environment.

These considerations suggest a rather unusual question. If, having no Greek, a reader wishes to sense something of the qualities of Homer, will he be better served by an English translation than by a translation into some other language? To avoid the obvious retort that it depends on his familiarity with the language chosen the question may be put in another form. What nation has the best chance of appreciating the magic of Homer if it reads only translations of Homer into its own language?

We shall discuss in the next chapter some of the advantages of German in translating; it is sufficient here to recall the difficulties encountered in the translation of Homer. If, despite Matthew Arnold's opinion, Homer cannot be successfully rendered in English hexameters, a greater satisfaction may possibly be found in a German version.

The *Iliad* was, in fact, translated into German hexameters by Johann Voss in 1793, and by J. Schroeder in 1854. The passage at the end of the Eighth Book, which was chosen by

Arnold as best for the purposes of comparison, is given by Voss in the following words:

Also zwischen des Xanthos Flut und den Schiffen Achaias
Leuchteten weit vor Ilios her die Feuer der Troer.
Tausende solche Feuer brannten im Felde; aber an jedem
Sassen fünfzig der Männer im Glanz des lodernden Feuers.
Doch die Rosse standen, mit Spelt und Gerste genähret,
Der schön thronenden Eos harrend, bei ihren Wagen.

Two things are obvious; one, which has always been recognized, that the German language is well fitted to the rhythm of the hexameter; secondly, that there is undoubtedly something about the German rendering that has escaped the English translation. It is something that gives the Greekless German reader a nearer approach to Homer than the Greekless Briton can easily attain.

Undeniably, there remains too great a tendency in thinking of the translation of poetry to overemphasize the apparent impossibility, for there is always an aspect of poetic writing which is neither words nor music nor memorable expression. This is the vision that prompts the poet's thoughts and which he tries to show us and to share with us. The poet has seen or heard or otherwise experienced something that we might never have known but for his poetry; and these experiences can be expressed in another tongue by simple and faithful translation.

To try to make this idea clear one may take examples from English poetry which could indeed be adequately put before other readers in other languages. They could be given the full force of the poet's vision, the peculiar way in which the poet apprehended reality.

The concluding passage of 'Sohrab and Rustum' is an outstanding example on a fairly large scale: one can so clearly see that in French, for instance, it would be no less striking, no less characteristic than it is in the poem we all know. In a shorter example, however, the effect may be more concentrated, more vivid. Flecker's wonderful

> A ship, an isle, a sickle moon.
> With few, but with how splendid stars ...

has something in it that would not be lost by translation, and all its memorable character would be preserved. And the same is true of Matthew Arnold's 'moon-blanched grass', visible to the mind of anyone who looks at his lawn by the light of the full moon. This function of poetry, the function of giving sharper perception, makes translation worth while.

VII

Translating modern languages

What is not clear is not French.
RIVAROL

Among the languages which an Englishman describes as foreign, French holds a position of its own. The long-standing relations between the French and the British, from the days when our Court was occupied by Frenchmen speaking their own language, down to the *entente cordiale* and a subsequent alliance in two German wars, have resulted in an intimacy which shows itself in countless ways, including our linguistic habits. To a very large number of Englishmen, the words 'going abroad' imply going to France much more inevitably than they suggest such alternatives as going to Germany or going to Spain. Whenever circumstances create a demand for linguists those who profess French only are so numerous that they find the market value of their accomplishment to be almost negligible, and their offer of service is likely to be dismissed with the remark, 'French? Would you call that a foreign language, exactly?' And in everyday life a hundred Englishmen may respond to a small surprise with the exclamation *'Mon Dieu'* for one who would say *'Mein Gott'*; a thousand for one who would ejaculate *'Tη καὶ θεοί'.*

Clearly, too, the French language possesses an individuality that does not appear to the same degree in other languages that have made contributions to the English tongue, so that in using or reading such familiar words as 'café', 'bureau', or 'bonhomie' the average man, uninterested in philology, thinks of them as being French in a way that he does not think of 'radius' as being Latin or 'diameter' as being Greek.

As the military power of Rome carried the boundaries of the Empire farther and farther over Europe, the Latin language was spread with it, influencing and being in its turn influenced by the speech of those living in the conquered and occupied countries. For reasons which are difficult now to discern, the Latin spoken in Northern Gaul changed more rapidly and more completely than that of other regions, with the result that among several Roman dialects that spoken by the Franks, and in particular the variety used in Paris, came to be adjudged as a distinct language, French. By A.D. 800 this language could boast a sufficient literature, and, so far as a language can be said o have a birth date, the ninth century is regarded as that of literary French.

Not unlike a human infant, the language developed rapidly at first, continuing to draw its nourishment from its Latin mother. Yet, after two hundred years, the inhibitions of adolescence seemed to make themselves felt; there arose by comparison almost a resistance to the intrusion of new words. Consequently, the difference between 'Early French' of the eleventh and twelfth centuries and modern French of the eighteenth and nineteenth centuries is much less pronounced than the difference between the Early and modern English of the same periods.

There is thus a conspicuous core of Latin ancestry in the French language and many French words have preserved a close relation to the meanings of their Latin origins. The English student of French is far from unfamiliar with words derived from Latin, and this may encourage him to hope for a consequent parallelism between French and English, which will make his study of the former much easier than it would otherwise have been. But his hope is short-lived; for this very community of origin is responsible for many of the difficulties in an accurate translation of French. Indeed, it would not be at all difficult to develop and support the thesis that French is one of the most difficult languages to put into English, especially if the translation is to be made with the highest standards of accuracy and literary quality.

The difficulties in translating French are derived from the different evolutionary histories of French and English. While French, resisting infiltration, was making the best use of its relatively limited vocabulary by allowing each word to acquire a clear, definite meaning, English was importing words from various sources, creating others, and developing into an essentially composite, not to say a heterogeneous, language with a larger vocabulary and a higher proportion of synonyms. Two results follow: French is a language that should be as clear and precise as classical Latin, English does not so readily achieve the same degree of clarity and precision when used by writers and speakers of a comparable degree of skill. In other words, it must always be harder for an Englishman to write the best English than for a Frenchman to write the best French; and in fact a smaller proportion of Englishmen do so.

The second consequence is the very marked difference between French and English in grammar, in idiom, and in the construction of a sentence. The following simple phrases, chosen almost at random, illustrate this:

Tout le monde	*Cela ne marche pas*
Comment ça va?	*Qu'est-ce que c'est que ça?*

In these, as in countless others, the literal sense can only be regarded as a paraphrase of the actual meaning.

There have always been students of philology who have used this and other peculiarities of French to deny its claim to an enhanced clearness, and have voiced the opinion that this is no more than a superstition, diligently cultivated by the French in their own interests. A paragraph from the autobiography of the late L. S. Amery, *My Political Life*,* typically puts forward this point of view. He wrote:

> To all Frenchmen their language is an idolized thing, their Holy of Holies. To pay due reverence to it, to dwell on its clarity, its precision, its felicity, will set any Frenchman purring, and in a mood to agree with almost any argument. To suggest that its vocabulary is very limited, has not even got words for 'to stand' or 'to lie', or for 'right' or 'wrong', and requires two words to say 'not' and eight words to say 'what is that' is a mortal insult. To speak French, however imperfectly, shows at least an appreciation of higher things. Not even to take the trouble to learn it marks the barbarian living in outer spiritual darkness.

What, then, is the sum of the effects of all these characteristics of the French language on the process of translation?

The first is undoubtedly the apparent and terribly deceptive similarity between so many words in the two languages. Many English words have entered our language from French, and many words have come into both English and French from the same Latin and Greek origins, so that there is a large group of words which occur in both languages in the same, or recognizably the same, form. If a translator assumes that these words have preserved the same meanings and if he has enough knowledge of French to enable him to translate most of the words which are unlike anything in English, words like *homme* and *cheval* and *chien*, he may, with some luck, be able to get a sort of idea of the contents of any passage. But it will not be accurate, and may even be far from what the original writer had intended.

* Hutchinson, 1953.

French, in fact, is full of examples of what has been called illusory correspondence, and the would-be translator is obliged to learn very soon that *brave* does not mean 'brave', *honnête* does not mean 'honest', *joli* does not mean 'jolly', and so on. Before long it becomes an article of faith that if a French word looks like an English word it is certain to have a different meaning.

Almost any passage of French prose will illustrate most of the characteristics of French translation; the paragraph chosen here is the opening of Félicien Marceau's novel, *L'Homme du Roi*:

> *Lorsqu'on passe maintenant rue des Arcades et qu'on la voit si animée, si bruyante, on a peine à imaginer qu'en 1921 encore, c'était une des rues les plus paisibles du quartier Nord. Le tramway 22 qui aujourd'hui la traverse n'existait pas, ni l'autobus rouge de la ligne Gare Centrale — Place des Palais. Les deux grands immeubles à appartements n'étaient pas encore construits. En fait de magasins, il n'y avait que la boulangerie, qui existe toujours, et un antiquaire. maintenant remplacé par la librairie anglaise.*

A translation of this is:

> It would be difficult for anyone going along the Arcade today, and finding such a busy, noisy street, to believe that even in 1921 it was one of the quietest roads in the north quarter. Tram 22, which now goes down it, did not exist, nor did the red bus from the Central Station to Palace Square. The two great blocks of flats were not built. As for shops, there were only the baker's, which is still there, and an antique shop, now replaced by the English book-seller's.

A comparison of these two extracts shows that to produce an easy, readable English paragraph the translator has had in almost every sentence to alter the exact construction. He has preserved the sense of the paragraph perfectly, and has given us the same impression of surprising change; but his words prove completely that anything like a literal translation of the French would not be anything like literary English.

If this is true of prose, how much more incisively is it true of French poetry, which is quite one of the most untranslatable forms of European literature. A few lines of French verse provide the most searching test of scholarship that can readily be found, but even the most satisfactory results support the opinion of Professor J. G. Weightman, who wrote that there is no translation of a French poem that conveys more than half the force of the original.

Whatever may be the differences of opinion, the best French is clear and precise, so that the problem before any translator is to be equally clear and precise in English, while accurately preserving the meaning of the original. To do this requires an intimate knowledge of French, as well as a knowledge of English superior to that of the average Englishman; and it also requires an expenditure of time and labour such as neither publisher nor reviewer would adequately reward.

The differences between the German and the French tongues are so many, so wide, and so deep that the two languages, both of which are moderately familiar to many Englishmen, might almost have been designed to enable writers on linguistic matters to find the examples they need to illustrate their ideas. French, we have just seen, is a difficult language, very different from English; it is also extremely musical, so that the sound of the voice of a Frenchwoman, heard on Radio-Paris, has a compelling charm which challenges the appeal of a violin. German, on the other hand, is closely related to English and so it is easier to learn. It is easier to read German without meeting verbal or

95

constructional problems than it is to read French: and it is easier to write German more or less as a German would write it than it is to write French like that of a Frenchman. Further, it is guttural, and often harsh; if French possesses the beauty of a violin, German has as little auditory appeal as a piano.

These facts about the nature of the German language, which are doubtless well-known to many, can be illustrated in a simple way which yields an unexpected result. In Chapter V the qualities of the Latin language were displayed by recalling Canon Hannay's words about its use in prayers, and in illustration the Third Collect of Evening Prayer was quoted.

Here are the French and German versions of the same appeal to 'Lighten our darkness'.

Illumine nos ténèbres, ô Seigneur; et par ta grande miséricorde garantis-nous de tous les dangers et de tous les accidents de cette nuit, pour l'amour de ton Fils unique, notre Sauveur Jésus-Christ.

Wir bitten dich, o Herr, erleuchte unsere Finsternis, und beschütze uns durch deine grosse Güte unter allen Gefahren dieser Nacht, um der Liebe deines einzigen Sohnes, unsere Heilandes, Jesu Christi, willen.

These are well worth reading attentively. The German lies as near to the Latin as does the English, and reads as smoothly; the French seems at first to approach the Latin too closely – *illumine* for *illumina, miséricorde* for *misericordiam* – and so to declare itself a language of different antecedents from English. This may be accepted, a consequence of what has always been obvious about the words of the French language; but when in the next phrase the writer asks to be 'guaranteed' against all 'accidents', then the widening gulf between the two tongues suggests an application for an insurance policy. This is admittedly unfortunate, except for our present purpose.

The examples quoted make it plain that whereas in French a word which resembles an English word seldom, if ever, has the same meaning, in German it is, in fact, more usually the same word. The phenomenon of 'deceptive resemblance' is rare between the English and the German languages; and this is the first reason for the smaller risk of errors in translation.

A second reason for the greater proportional accuracy of the mediocre translator of German lies in the more rigid construction of the German sentence. There is customarily much less variation between the many sentences on a page of German prose than may be found on a page of English or French, where sentences are usually different both in mode of construction and in individual length. This relative constancy makes it easier to enunciate definite principles for translating German into English, and then to achieve a good translation by applying them. To take as an example no more than the very elementary rule which applies to the translating of verbs of varying moods and tenses, one may quote the familiar fact that 'for every word in German there must be a corresponding word in English'. If the final form is something like 'it shall have been said', then it should be true that the four words 'shall' and 'have' and 'been' and 'said' have been written because there were four words, not three and not five, in the German. If a simple rule like this were applied to a French sentence the result would resemble the caricature written by Mark Twain and quoted in Chapter II.

This correspondence helps to justify the statement, found in a German Technical Reader, that 'translation from German into English can largely be reduced to a scientific formula'. Such a statement as this is probably very near the truth when reference is made to technical writings in which style has a secondary place, and even in literary works the principles which produced it will be found to be operating.

These are the chief reasons for which linguists in general find less to say, less to discuss and less to baffle them in the matter of German translation than they do when writing about some other languages: in a word German seldom produces the same proportion of problems and difficulties as are found in French and Latin. This must not be taken to imply that there are no paragraphs in German prose which do not test the skill and ingenuity of a translator, but they are not so likely to occur on every other page.

A passage of literary German must be found and used to illustrate these points, as far as a single short passage can do so, and as an example Goethe's first impression of Strassburg, taken from his book, *Aus Meinem Leben*, has been chosen.

Und so sah ich denn ... die ansehliche Stadt, die weitumher-liegenden, mit herrlichen dichten Blumen besetzten und durch-flochtenen Auen, diesen auffallenden Reichtum der Vegetation, der, dem Laufe des Rheins folgend, die Ufer, Inseln, und Werder bezeichnet. Nicht weniger mit mannigfaltigem Grün geschmückt ist der von Süden herab sich ziehende flache Grund, welchen die Iller bewässert; selbst westwärts nach dem Gebirge zu finden sich manche Niederungen, die einen ebenso reizenden Anblick von Wald und Wiesenwuchs gewähren, sowie nördliche, mehr hügeliche Teil von unendlichen kleinen Bächen durch-schnitten ist, die überall ein schnelles Wachstum begünstigen.

This is translatable thus:

And then I saw the considerable town, the fields decked and mingled with magnificent flowers, a striking luxuri-ance of plant life, which, following the course of the

Rhine, marks its banks, islands and islets. The plain, running up from the south and watered by the Iller, is decorated with a no less varied green; westwards, towards the mountains, it forms the lowlands that make an equally delightful vista of forest and meadow; while to the north the broken hills are intersected by countless little streams, encouraging rapid growth everywhere.

There is no justification for the idea that the translation of German is uninteresting, or that it has no part to play in discussions of the translator's art. The suggestion that those who know no Greek should read Homer in German has been made in Chapter V, but it was based there on no more than the fact that the German language lends itself to the composition of hexameters. The further truth is that German has qualities that make it, when competently handled, a language into which others may often be satisfactorily translated, or, more particularly, can be more faithfully and successfully translated than into any other.

Most, if not all, of the plays of Shakespeare have been translated into French, and in France they have met with a reception characterized by interest rather than enthusiasm. Shakespeare has also been translated into German, and so successful has been the translation that at one time it used to be said, probably with truth, that Shakespeare was better appreciated and more often produced on the stage in Germany than in his native country. There may well be reasons other than linguistic for the difference between the two opinions of an English dramatist, but there cannot be much doubt that the language itself takes a share in emphasizing it.

One of the most illuminating examples of this feature of German is to be found in Strodtmann's translation of Tennyson's song in 'The Princess'. The first stanza is enough to

99

show that the translator has been able to reproduce the metre, the arrangement of rhymes and even the masculine and feminine rhyming.

> The splendour falls on castle walls
>> And snowy summits old in story:
> The long light shakes across the lakes,
>> And the wild cataract leaps in glory.
> Blow, bugle, blow, set the wild echo flying,
> Blow, bugle, answer echoes, dying, dying, dying.

> *Es fällt der Strahl auf Berg und Thal*
>> *Und schneeige Gipfel, reich an Sagen:*
> *Viel' Lichter wehn auf blauen Seen,*
>> *Bergab die Wasserstürze jagen.*
> *Blas, Hüfthorn, blas, in Wiederhall erschallend,*
> *Blas, Horn; antwortet Echos, hallend, hallend, hallend.*

During the years immediately following the First World War there were made some of the most successful attempts to broaden the educational horizon, especially because this horizon had confined and cramped the public and secondary schools. For example, in many schools biology was for the first time offered to would-be medical students, and was welcomed because it enabled a boy to enter a Medical School with the First M.B. behind him, a year to the good.

On the Modern Side the new arrival was Spanish, supported by a growing importance in the world of industry and with this the reputation, which it quickly acquired, of being an 'easy' language to learn.*

To learn a language, or anything else, thoroughly and systematically, so that a degree of mastery is obtained, is seldom likely to be easy, but students discovered, and have ever since exploited, a feature of Spanish that particularly

* See Note 3.

appealed to them, namely that it is an easy language to learn imperfectly. This gives it a scholastic value which enhances its popularity, for various seats of learning require of their entrants such qualifications as 'a language other than English' or 'Latin and one approved alternative language'. In such circumstances Spanish was to the non-linguist what biology was to the non-mathematical, an officially approved soft option.

In consequence, Spanish in British schools has never looked back since the day of its introduction. It is a language which shows a peculiarity that cannot easily be matched elsewhere, the fact that about one-quarter of those who speak it live in the country of its origin, while the remaining three-quarters live in the western hemisphere and speak a Spanish that is noticeably different from pure Castilian.

The history of the evolution of the language is closely comparable to the evolution of French, and scholars have been able to trace with an approach to continuity the steps that led from the speech in common use at the time of the Roman Empire to the matured language of today.

Spain was occupied for about two hundred years from 201 B.C.; that is to say earlier than the invasion of Southern Gaul in 123 B.C., Northern Gaul in 58 B.C., or Britain in 55 B.C. The language grew from the idiomatic speech, or from what is sometimes called vulgar Latin, of the soldiers and traders, a conversational Latin, rather different from the more refined Latin of literature. Its development was guided by the Roman genius for the making of roads: no fewer than thirty-four great Roman roads can still be detected in Spain, crossing the land in all directions; and at one time they took the Latin language over the whole country.

In consequence, about 65 per cent of the Spanish vocabulary is directly derived from Latin, a proportion that may be compared with 10 per cent from Greek and 8 per cent from German and Arabic, while there are many Spanish words of Latin origin whose counterparts are not found in French or Italian. Examples are *cieno*, mud; *cordero*, lamb; *miedo*, fear; and *puchero*, saucepan. The tendency to retain a final vowel is evident here, but Spanish quickly shed the declension of nouns and merged all the cases in one.

There has always been a tendency in Spain to recognize different dialects in different regions of the country. The official Castilian Spanish took on its present form during the sixteenth century, the National Library of Spain was founded by Philip V in 1711, and the Real Academia di la Lengua in 1713. This body produced a massive six-volume dictionary between 1726 and 1739.

A Swedish philologist, Dr F. Wulff, has described Spanish as the most emphatic, the most harmonious, the most elegant and the most expressive of all the neo-Latin languages. With such a reputation it is much to be regretted that it is undeniably open to rather facile translations, such as would scarcely be perpetrated or accepted in the case of any other modern language. As an example of this, reference may be made to the most popular of all Spanish books, the *Adventures of Don Quixote*, of 1605. Of it Woodhouselee said that there is no book to which it is harder to do justice in translation. This is a serious comment, and it is supported by its writer in a whole chapter devoted to comparison and comment on the two translations made by Motteux and Smollett. A short example will suffice to show how different were the versions of the two translators, differences which caused Woodhouselee to discuss them at considerable length.

It will be recalled that Don Quixote, having got the worst of a brawl, was laid on a wretched bed in a loft:

En esta maldita cama se acostó Don Quijote, y luego la Ventera
y su hija le emplastaron de arriba abajo, alumbrándoles

Maritornes, que así se llamaba la asturiana. Y como al bismalle viese la Ventera tan acardenalado a partes a Don Quijote, dijo que aquello más parecían golpes que caída.

In this ungracious bed was the Knight laid to rest his belaboured carcase; and presently the hostess and her daughter anointed and plastered him all over, while Maritornes, for that was the name of the Asturian wench, held the candle. The hostess, while she greased him, wondering to see him so bruised all over, I fancy, said she, those bumps look much more like a dry beating than a fall. (Motteux)

In this wretched bed Don Quixote, having laid himself down, was anointed from head to foot by the good woman and her daughter, while Maritornes (that was the Asturian's name) stood hard by, holding a light. The landlady, in the course of her application, perceiving the Knight's whole body black and blue, observed, that those marks seemed rather the effects of a drubbing than of a fall. (Smollett)

Woodhouselee tells us that Smollett actually based his work on a previous translation made by Jarvis, trying first to improve a rather rough and crude version, and secondly to avoid any of the expressions used by Motteux. This often involved the rejection of words and phrases which were apt and their replacement by others not so suitable, so that, on the whole, Smollett's translation is inferior to Motteux's.

In conclusion, and as a supplement to the above, there follows a Spanish translation of the Collect for Aid against All Perils, which reads as follows:

A clara nuestras tinieblas, suplicámoste Oh Señor: y por tu gran misericordia, defiéndenos de todos los temores y peligros de esta noche: por amor de tu único Hijo, nuestro Salvador Jesucristo.

This should be compared with the French and German translations already given, but above all, the comparison should, if possible, be made by reading the three aloud. The consequence is inevitably to recall the comparison which asserts that a man should speak Spanish to his God, French to his friends, German to his enemies, and Italian to his mistress. To this there has been added the opinion that for any or all of these purposes Russian is equally suitable, for, so it is claimed, it possesses the majesty of Spanish, the vivacity of French, the strength of German and the sweetness of Italian, with, for good measure, the richness of Latin and Greek also. Regretfully, this comprehensive claim cannot be examined here; and with equal regret there may be noticed the absence of English from this list of the elect.*

* See Note 4.

VIII

Translating the Bible

So great is the force of established usage that even acknowledged corruptions please the greater part, for they prefer to have their copies pretty rather than accurate.

JEROME

Among our present studies the translation of the Bible holds an important, indeed a unique, position. There are two chief reasons for this.

The first and the more fundamental is that the subject matter of the Bible, and especially of the Old Testament, touches man's very existence; it tells him about his origin, his purpose and his destination. For countless generations men have been advised to seek the reason for their lives in the pages of the Bible, and to draw from the same source the rules by which these lives ought to be governed; they have absorbed this instruction at impressionable ages, so that many of them have grown up with the doctrines of the Bible woven into their emotional constitutions. The Bible has become in a real sense different from all other books, and with this it has become untouchable. Men have sought in its pages comfort, or inspiration, or strength, and have found these blessings emotionally rather than logically offered them. This is what they have preferred, so that their religious attitude rests on an unshakeable faith, in which they will permit no alteration. The cold logic of any thinker who, in fact, may seek to do no more than to underline the difference between beliefs that are based on emotion and tenets that are demonstrable facts is likely to be received, and has often been received, with a storm of opposition and abuse as unjustified as it is unjustifiable.

The second reason for the unique position of the Bible text among translations is of course the unapproachable quality of the text of the Authorized Version. This has been praised so often, so universally, and for so long that there is no need, at this point, to do more than recall the fact. Yet from this there follows the consequence that the English-speaking peoples, having grown up with it, are inclined, normally and naturally, if like most people they are normal and natural and not rational, to resent any suggestion of change in its matchless words and phrases. No other translators have to face this position: that there already exists a magnificent example of the very work to which they have set their hands, a version so beloved, so enshrined in the hearts of their readers, that they can hope to improve it, here and there, only in matters of editorial detail.

From the point of view of the student of translation the Bible is peculiar in that it has for long been known as a translation. The earliest manuscripts have either perished or have not yet been discovered. There is evidence that an established Hebrew text of the Old Testament was in use at the end of the first century A.D., and that from it were derived both the Greek version known as the Septuagint, the earliest parts of which may date back to the third century, and, in the fourth century, the Latin version known as the Vulgate.

The Vulgate was the work of Eusebius Hieronymus, more usually known as St Jerome, the finest scholar of his age and the first to make a translation of the whole Bible into Latin. His aim was to keep to the wording of his predecessors whenever this seemed to him to be accurate, and to introduce changes only where corruption of the text was apparent. His translation has long been regarded as one of the three supreme versions, fit to be compared with Luther's German Bible and our own King James's Version. It continued in general use in Britain until the time of the Reformation.

A very large number of English translations of the Bible have been made in the last six hundred years, and they may be considered in three ways: as fragments of historical bibliography; as part of the development of theological doctrine; and as a series of examples of translational practice. Each of these has its place in the growth of literary scholarship: in this chapter the translating must be given emphasis over the other aspects.

As a preliminary point, attention should be called to the fact, peculiar to Bible translating, that over the years there have been changes in our knowledge of the original texts, changes in our knowledge of the Hebrew and ancient Greek languages, and changes in our use of our own language. Translators of other books do not expect to have to meet the first two of these vital characteristics of Bible translation.

The first English version was due to the conviction of John Wyclif (? 1320–82), Master of Balliol and Canon of Lincoln, that men could be expected to order their lives in accordance with the precepts of the Bible only if they were able to read the book itself. He was probably not the actual translator; the work, based on the Vulgate, was done by his friends. There were two versions: the earlier is believed to have been made largely by Nicholas of Hereford in 1382, and the second, a revision, was edited by John Purvey, who had been Wyclif's secretary, in 1390.

The first translation, following Wyclif's advice, was a very literal translation; it often preserved the word order and the Latin constructions of the Vulgate, even when the consequence was not good English. Purvey, however, is believed to have compared several Latin manuscripts, and, defending his method, produced a more natural text.

At this time the Bible, like every other book, was written by hand and so could be reproduced only by the laborious process of copying. The scribes who undertook this task were always liable to make mistakes, a form of human frailty which has been responsible for countless uncertainties in all the earliest manuscripts.

The first printed Bible was the work of William Tyndale (? 1484–1536), and was not made from the Vulgate but from the Greek of Erasmus. Tyndale believed that the quality of the English was of greater importance than literal faithfulness. He began to make his translation about 1523, when he was living in London, but found it advisable to move to Germany. Here, first at Cologne and later at Worms, he completed the printing of the New Testament in 1526. This was followed in 1530 by the Pentateuch, translated from the Hebrew.

Tyndale had not finished the Old Testament at the time of his martyrdom, and in 1535 the first complete printed English Bible was produced at Cologne by Miles Coverdale (1488–1569). He used German and Latin texts since he knew neither Greek nor Hebrew, and he often followed Tyndale closely.

Tyndale had left a quantity of manuscript translations of parts of the Old Testament, and these were taken by one of his followers, John Rogers, added to the existing Tyndale version, and a composite work completed by using the necessary parts of Coverdale. The whole was produced at Antwerp under the pseudonymous editorship of Thomas Matthew in 1537. Two years later it was re-edited by Richard Taverner.

In 1538 Cromwell ordered that every church should contain a Bible for general use, and to meet the demand a revision of the Matthew Bible was made by Coverdale. It was known as the Great Bible and is most familiar to us today because it contained the Psalms as they still appear in our Book of Common Prayer. It is sometimes called Cranmer's Bible because he wrote a preface to the edition of 1540.

The famous Geneva Bible appeared in 1560. It was the

work of William Whittingham, John Knox, and others who were determined to further the doctrine of Protestantism. This was the Bible of Shakespeare, and it was a great and popular success. Its rendering of Genesis iii, 7, 'and they sowed fig-tree leaves together and made themselves breeches', has caused it to be affectionately known as the Breeches Bible.

The reception, favourable or antagonistic, given to all these Bibles from Tyndale's onwards, was determined not by their literary standards but by the doctrinal character of the included 'Notes'. It was because Archbishop Parker disapproved of the Puritan notes to the Geneva Bible, and was also dissatisfied with the Great Bible, that he caused a panel of bishops to edit another version. This, appropriately known as the Bishops' Bible, appeared in 1568. It was not so much a new translation as a re-writing of the Geneva Bible, and it remained the authoritative Bible of the Church in Britain for forty-three years.

At about the same time members of the Roman Catholic Church felt the need to produce a Bible of their own. Translations of the New Testament, published in 1582, and of the Old Testament in 1609 were the work of Professor Gregory Martin of the English College of Douai and (temporarily) of Rheims. They were based on the Vulgate and contain a proportion of Latinisms which do not tend towards easy reading. A typical feature, interesting from the point of view of translation, is its version of the Psalms. The psalms in the Vulgate were based on a Gallican psalter from the Greek Septuagint: hence the Douai psalter is a translation of a translation of a translation. We have met this phenomenon before. Although the Douai-Rheims Bible more than once received editorial attention, it was due for a complete revision by the eighteenth century, and this was undertaken by Bishop Richard Challoner. He produced several successive revisions of his own work which finally took the form of the Douai Bible as in use, with minor emendations, today.

On 14th January, 1603, King James I summoned the bishops and other clergy to a conference at Hampton Court. On the following day Dr John Reynolds, President of Corpus Christi, Oxford, and Dean of Lincoln, put forward this plea: 'May your Majesty be pleased that the Bible be new translated, such as are extant not answering the original?' To this the King agreed, saying, 'I confess I could never yet see a Bible well translated in English; but I think that of all, that of Geneva is the worst.' Here and thus was the birth of the Authorized Version.

In July of the following year the forty-seven learned men were appointed, and three years later began their work, which was published by the King's Printer in 1611. The Bishops' Bible was the foundation, and reference was freely made to the other translations mentioned above as well as to Greek and Hebrew texts. King James had supplied a set of rules which were to be observed, and the translators adopted the principle of giving their readers the spirit and meaning of their 'originals' in preference to a closer translation. They were especially careful of the rhythm and euphony of their work, and in this their success has never been approached.

As a literary achievement the Authorized Version is unlikely to be superseded by any other as long as the English language is spoken or read, a claim that can hardly be made for any other translation in the literature of the world.

Like all its predecessors, the Authorized Version received its share of criticism. Where the critics found fault with its scholarship they deserved attention, and although new translations of several books were made during the next two centuries it was not until 1870 that the Bishop of Winchester, addressing the Upper House of Convocation, suggested the appointment of a committee to produce what is now known as the Revised Version. The New Testament was published in 1881, the Old Testament in 1884, and the Apocrypha in 1895. Praise for the Revised Version has always been couched in guarded terms. It was, as it was meant to be, an improved rendering of the Greek text, for which reason it has been widely approved in colleges and used by students, because its textual accuracy outweighs other features. It cannot be read with the same sensuous pleasure: put shortly, it is an example of what has already been described as 'translator's English'.

An edition of the Revised Version with modifications more acceptable to American opinion was published in 1901 and was known as the American Standard Version. It was protected by copyright which was acquired in 1928 by the International Council of Religious Education, and in due course this body determined on a revision. A committee of thirty-two scholars began work in 1937; they did not attempt a new translation, but a new version based on its predecessors of 1611, 1881 and 1901, with due consideration given to most recent opinions. The New Testament was published in 1946 and the two Testaments together in 1952 – the Standard Revised Version.

Its welcome was surprising and was deserved. English readers on both sides of the Atlantic appreciated the fact that here was the Bible in good literary English, unspoilt by Americanisms and free from such obsolescent words as 'saith' and 'thou'. It was really the first of the twentieth-century Bibles which seemed to promise 'to do for today and tomorrow what the Authorized Version did for the seventeenth and following centuries'. Criticism was nearly all based on doctrinal points, and an actual test conducted on 1,358 children in Ohio proved that it was more readily and accurately understood than was the Authorized Version. A translator unconcerned with doctrine could wish for nothing better.

Many readers will be surprised to learn that between 1902 and 1966 at least twenty-eight versions of the Bible, or at any rate of considerable parts of it, were produced in the English language. Why did this happen? No translator of the Bible can hope to produce a greater literary masterpiece than the Authorized Version, and in consequence there is reason for an examination of the hopes and ideals of modern translators.

One cannot begin such an examination without recalling the universal, fundamental and wholly natural tendency among all peoples to prefer the language in which they read Holy Writ to be slightly archaic, old-fashioned if it please you, slightly different from the language of the market-place or even of the study, slightly mysterious in phrase and in image. All such people will read 'And the veil of the Temple was rent in twain' with far greater satisfaction than its modern paraphrase: 'And the curtain in the Temple was torn in half.'

Obviously the Authorized Version satisfies these desires. Equally obviously there are many who sincerely believe that the message of the Bible can only be understood, appreciated, and in the literal sense assimilated into the reader's character if it is put before him in the plain speech of modern times. Translators who share this opinion do not hope to do more than to produce a version in acceptable English, fit to be considered as a reasonable alternative to the Authorized Version. Their belief must be that they are making the Bible easier to read, and that they are thereby increasing the number of its readers, a wholly laudable object.

Others are evidently working under the inspiration of scholarship. Learning and scholarship continuously improve our knowledge of the earliest sources of the Bible text and also of the languages in which it was written, so that we are becoming increasingly aware that in the traditional versions there are mistakes which can be corrected, obscure passages that need no longer remain difficult, and preferable readings to passages which at one time seemed to offer alternatives. These defects, and others, scholarship is now prepared to remove or reduce, to present us with a version of the Bible which is written in modern English and is accurate because it tells us, as nearly as is possible, what the original authors really meant us to read.

In an attempt to estimate fairly the results of revision, the principle of reader-analysis, used elsewhere, may helpfully be repeated, asking the question, Why does anyone read the Bible? The readers may be divided into the following groups:

(i) The clergy and the theological students, who must always maintain a professional concern for the Bible, which fills the place of their fundamental textbook.

(ii) The devout men and women who lead Christian lives, and who read the Bible regularly in the course of their devotions.

(iii) Less regular readers who are, however, likely at any time to read a few verses, a page, or a chapter, solely for their own satisfaction.

(iv) All the members of the congregations in churches and chapels, to whom the Bible is read aloud in public worship.

The first group hardly enters the present discussion, for professors are expected to know as much as possible of their subject, and like all scholars must keep abreast of its progress. But the facts remain that, first, a striving after scholarly accuracy is largely discounted by the absence of any in-disputably accurate original Hebrew or Greek versions. The available sources are not 'original', they are copies, or copies of copies of copies, and all of them different and inaccurate and puzzling in various degrees. The maker of a really new translation has to choose between a number of imperfect sources, and in places of divergence he has to choose the one he prefers, or condemn them all and make his own emendation.

The second question asks how great is the appeal of pure scholarship in the world of today; what is its place, if any, in the Welfare State? One has not heard the bishops and archbishops loudly proclaiming from the episcopal pulpits the virtues of the latest translations, nor asking for their general use in their dioceses. And yet, since bishops may not illogically be supposed to represent in general the scholarly element in what is essentially a learned vocation, their doing so would be a justification of the scholars' views, and would support the idea that scholarly accuracy in the text of the scriptures was of overwhelming importance.

The fourth group does not ask for much space, for its members have little opportunity to express their opinions on what is read to them, or to state their wishes as to what should be read. This leaves the second and third groups, which are much the largest, and therefore the most important for the translator who wishes to reach the hearts and minds of his readers. The fundamental fact about both the devout and the casual readers is that nearly all of them learned to know and to love the Authorized Version during the impressionable years of childhood. This is of overwhelming importance; all that is contained and implied in the phrase 'at their mother's knee' colours the whole of their Bible reading. The conservatism of children is well known; and it is a characteristic of all human minds that they resent and oppose change. That their opposition may be illogical, their resentment indefensible, and their whole attitude obstructionist, is of no significance, for their attitude is universal and constitutes a real factor in human progress in every sort of human activity.

But there are others, and their name is legion, who form indeed the greater part of the rising generation. When Sir Arthur Quiller-Couch spoke of the prose of the Authorized Version, he said, 'It is in everything we see, hear, feel, because it is in us, in our blood.'

These words occur at the end of a lecture which he gave in May 1913. Read today, more than half a century later, they might easily evoke the comment 'It sure is not'. And this is true. The generation that learned of the Bible at their mothers' knees has been replaced by another; mothers have been more variously employed and their knees have found different functions. Their children have changed accordingly. At one time it was said that we do less than justice to the newer translations if we conclude that they have improved those parts of the Bible that nobody wants to read and have failed to leave those parts that everybody reads in the form in which all will continue to do so; but opinions also change, and the Bibles of the present century deserve a sympathetic consideration.

A survey of all these Bibles shows the uniform intention of making the book more freely read by the multitude. The example was set by Dr J. Weymouth, whose *New Testament in Modern Speech* in 1903 was the first undoubtedly successful attempt to present the gospels and epistles in the language of contemporary Englishmen. Other versions at about the same time were not so popular, and this may have been in part due to Weymouth's scholarly yet balanced point of view. He said that 'without a tinge of antiquity it is scarcely possible that there should be that dignity of style that befits the sacred themes'. Clearly, the operative word is 'tinge', implying that the antiquity must not be obtrusive; and this opinion survives to the present day, for we have been told by Dr Alexander Jones of Liverpool that in forfeiting 'biblical language' we lose something that is 'very precious'.

There are detectable three distinct genera of twentieth-century Bibles. The most primitive are the simple paraphrases that have aimed at nothing more than plain, modern English, with little or no concern for textual accuracy. The most daring fall into the category of pseudo-translation, discussed in Chapter XIII, and in reading them one wonders what their successors will be like in a hundred years' time. The temptation is irresistible to prophesy that our descendants may open the first chapter of Genesis and read: 'Well, to start with, God made the earth and the sky; the earth was misshapen and empty and dark everywhere ... and he said "Let's have a light here" ... "Ah, that's good."'

The second genus, which is commendably the largest, contains real new translations made by real scholars, driven by devotion and enthusiasm. Many of these reach a surprisingly large number of readers, and their translators are deservedly rewarded. There is always great interest in noting and comparing the short expositions of their principles which the translators have included in their prefaces. And these differ. Dr James Moffatt, for example, whose New Testament was published in 1913 and Old Testament in 1924, wished to 'present the books of the Old and the New Testaments in effective, intelligible English'. Monsignor Ronald Knox, whose translation has been received by the Roman Catholic Church as a worthy companion, or perhaps a successor, to the Douai Bible, aimed at a 'timeless, acceptable' English; and the Reverend J. B. Phillips, whose successes in this sphere have been the most spectacular, set himself the seemingly impossible task of 'forgetting' the Authorized Version and translating the Greek Testament 'as if it were new'.

Obviously, there is nothing to prevent anyone from re-opening the familiar Greek Testament, with which in years gone by he gained admission to Oxford or Cambridge, and setting about the same task, and, in fact, a number of men have done so. The most significant differences are to be found between the theologians, whose practical knowledge of Greek is almost limited to the New Testament, and those who have a classical scholar's wider familiarity with the literature of ancient Greece.

The third and most sophisticated genus contains the new translations made by committees of scholars, made slowly and with the greatest possible care, with reference to and comparisons of the most trustworthy of the ancient scripts. In our generation nothing has approached the New English Bible and the Jerusalem Bible.

A suggestion that a completely new translation of the Bible should be undertaken was made at the General Assembly of the Church of Scotland in 1946. The idea met with general approval, a committee was formed in the following year, and, meeting in Westminster Abbey under Bishop Hunkin of Truro, appointed three panels of translators and a fourth panel of literary advisers. General director of the whole enterprise was Professor C. H. Dodd of Cambridge.

The panels worked slowly, with constant interchange of drafts, corrections and opinions; and the version of the New Testament was approved in March 1960, representing thirteen years' work.

Professor Dodd has told us of the principles and ideals that the translators had set before themselves. They wished to produce a Bible which should be an accurate transcription of the best authenticated texts, which should be scholarly with no trace of pedantry, which above all should be couched in modern English idiom with a preference for short and simple sentences; and which should be equally suitable for reading aloud or for private study. If this were accomplished, they hoped that the New English Bible would be universally accepted as an authoritative translation, and one which would encourage many to become more familiar with the words and doctrines of the scriptures.

Immediately on its publication the New English Bible received the widespread examination that was only to be expected, and Dr D. Nineham has done valuable service by editing a large collection of these reviews. They show, inevitably, a large number of individual comments on isolated words and phrases, most of which are negligible since there is no reason to suppose that the critics were better scholars than the translators. As a work of translation the New English Bible has received more care from competent scholars than had any of its predecessors: it is undoubtedly more easily read by the 'ordinary man' who does not know the Authorized Version particularly well, and is therefore likely to achieve its aim of producing a better and more widespread appreciation of the fundamentals of Christianity. The theologians have been more generous in their early assessments than have the purely literary critics; they have praised its faithfulness to the original Greek, and have especially commended the way in which it succeeds in bringing out the differences between the styles of the different books. This is an uncommon virtue in Bible translations: there is a tendency to translate as if all four gospels had been written in faultless, literary Greek of their time, whereas they were written in more colloquial styles, and with different feelings and purposes.

The New English Bible is a welcome expression of contemporary opinion among theologians, and as such it is of the greatest value to students. Laymen have freely found fault with it, largely because it lacks the lilt and rhythm of the Authorized Version. Yet they have applauded its approach to 'the current speech of our time' and the abandonment of any foredoomed attempt to design a 'timeless' English, when there can be no such language.

The book is reported to have sold six million copies in its first four years, proof, if proof were needed, that it is a really great achievement in an age in which neither Christianity nor scholarship is even moderately conspicuous. It is therefore worth recording the creation of a by-product of the translator's labours in the form of a revised text of the Greek New Testament, edited by Dr R. V. G. Tasker.

While we are awaiting the Old Testament of the New English Bible the gap is filled by the publication of the Old Testament of the Jerusalem Bible in 1966. This very large volume takes its name from the School of Biblical Studies, where some years ago a group of Dominican scholars undertook a translation of the Hebrew and Greek texts into French. *La Bible de Jérusalem* was an unqualified success all over France and in other Roman Catholic countries.

The English version was also a new translation, made by English Catholics from the same sources and continuously compared with its French counterpart, a method of production that has had no precedent in translating. Readers and reviewers alike have praised the style of the translation with a surprising consistency, and there can be no doubt that this version appears in delightful and lucid English. Moreover, it reflects more than might be expected of the poetry of the poetical books and passages.

A final appraisal of so many translations covering so long a period of time is as nearly impossible as can be imagined, yet a few thoughts seem to be clear.

The whole period from 1382 to 1966 has been one of almost continuous correction and revision, and there is no reason to suppose that this correction and revision will ever cease. Changes in our knowledge of the ancient languages occur and modify belief as to the nearest equivalents of various words and phrases. More rapidly our own language changes, both in the associations of words and the effects of idioms, so that what was once a good translation may become an incongruous one a decade or two later. Moreover, the readers differ. The historically minded may find satisfaction in the books of the Old Testament; the lovers of poetry, even though it be translated poetry, may share this satisfaction in the poetical books, and while the devout will want little beyond the gospels, the mystics may turn to the Revelation and the academic students to the sometimes involved words of St Paul. To make an ideal all-purposes Bible is probably as difficult or as impossible as to find a universally satisfying ideal in any other facet of human activity.

IX

Translation in action

The stark hopelessness of reproducing Horace.
SIR RONALD STORRS

Quintus Horatius Flaccus, the finest writer of the lyric that
the world has known, was born, the son of a collector of
taxes, on the border of Apulia on December 8th, 65 B.C. He
was educated in Rome and at the age of twenty went to
Athens for the study of philosophy. Returning to Rome in
41 B.C. he became a friend of Virgil, and was fortunate in
attracting the attention of Maecenus, a generous patron of
literature after the manner of the time. Some eight years
later Maecenus presented Horace with the Sabine Farm,
that recurs so often in his poetry, about twenty-five miles
from Rome; and here he found both independence and
contentment. His Odes, Books I to III, were offered to the
readers of Rome in 23 B.C. Horace died on November 27th
in his fifty-seventh year.

Of all the poets of antiquity Horace offers the most vivid
challenge to translators, who have willingly accepted the
opportunity of exposing their inability to achieve the impossible. Yet their attempts are so many, so varied, and
withal so sincere that an effort to collect and compare several
versions of one chosen passage has been found to be one of
the most illuminating ways of demonstrating a large proportion of the difficulties of translation.

The field of choice is a wide one, and I do not try
to rationalize my own attraction to the picture of the
poet, wandering afar, dreaming of his Lalage, careless of

danger and confident of his unshakeable love for his merry chatterbox.

The ode, number 22 in the First Book, which begins:

Integer vitae sclerisque purus
non eget Mauris iaculis neque arcu

and consists of six stanzas, is addressed to one Fuscus, a friend of Horace. In it the poet declares that the man who is upright and guiltless has no need for the protection of weapons wherever he may be. He supports his assertion by recalling that once, when he was walking far from his farm, an enormous wolf had fled from his presence. Then, changing his theme, he says that whether in frigid cold or tropic heat his thoughts will turn to his beloved Lalage.

This concluding sentiment occupies the fifth and sixth stanzas, which are quite sufficient for our purpose.

Pone me pigris ubi nulla campis
arbor aestiva recreatur aura,
quod latus mundi nebulae malusque
Iuppiter urget;

pone sub curru nimium propinqui
solis in terra domibus negata
dulce ridentem, Lalagen amabo,
dulce loquentem.

As we have already established, the first thing to be done in an attempt to translate this is to decide what Horace has said. The question of how he has said it must wait. We have also determined the function of a prose translation of a poem: it is a guide to show us how the Latin must be construed. Perhaps it cannot be more than this, but as such it is a first essential: and we shall therefore begin with a word-for-word construe, such as any Fifth Form boy or girl might be expected to produce.

Pone me, Place me; *pigris campis,* in unfruitful plains; *ubi nulla arbor,* where no tree; *recreatur,* is reawakened; *aestiva aura,* by the wind of summer; *latus mundi,* a side of the world; *quod nebulae,* which clouds; *malusque Iuppiter,* and evil Jupiter; *urget,* oppresses; *pone,* place; *sub curru solis,* under the chariot of the sun; *nimium propinqui,* too near; *in terra,* in a land; *negata,* denied; *domibus,* to homes; *amabo,* I shall love; *dulce ridentem,* sweetly smiling; *dulce loquentem,* sweetly speaking; *Lalagen,* Lalage.*

The first way in which this needs improvement is by giving more careful thought to the appropriate meanings of some of the words. In the passage there are at least six words whose nearest equivalents are elusive, and which require a little search before they are determined. They are: *pigris, recreatur, nebulae, malus, domibus, negata.*

(i) *Piger* is used in two senses. Of persons it means 're-luctant, unwilling'; of things, 'unfruitful, barren, or sterile'. In this context I think that 'barren' is the best.

(ii) *Recreatur* is 'recreated, reawakened, or brought again to life and action'. I think that 'revived' expresses this better than 'reawakened' or 'refreshed'.

(iii) *Nebula* is a mist or fog, just as a nebulous idea is an idea which is half-developed and not yet clear to the mind's eye. 'Cloud' is often used by translators of this ode, but cloud is not, in fact, given by some dictionaries. Clouds are often beautiful and may be impressive, *nebula* has no such association.

(iv) *Malus* is primarily bad, in the sense of 'mischievous, destructive, injurious'. These words are not suitable for the sky; but 'malicious' or 'malign', both of which are derived from it, express its implication more closely.

(v) *Domibus*: it is scarcely possible to decide between

* This is an accurate reproduction of an actual 'construe' made for me by a young student, unconscious of how he was being exploited.

'homes' and 'houses'. *Domus* is used in both senses and translators are equally divided between them. The rather intense associations of 'home' belong more to the British than to the Latin character, so that I would choose 'houses' rather than 'homes'.

(vi) *Negata*: *nego* has two meanings: primarily 'I say no' or 'deny', secondarily 'I refute' or 'decline'. To find the best word to stand for it when it qualifies a thing is not easy. 'Denied to houses' is too crude. I feel that the happiest solution to the problem is that offered by Lonsdale and Lee, who wrote 'Where dwellings may not be'. This correctly implies that houses cannot be built there, but by using 'may not' instead of 'cannot' preserves the idea of a verbal forbidding. Its disadvantage lies in the number of words it uses, but this is no worse than using fewer words that seem to be ill-chosen.

After stating these opinions the logical procedure is to put them into practice and write a prose translation which contains them:

> Place me in barren plains, where no tree is revived by the summer breeze, a part of the world which mists and a malign sky oppress; place me under the too-close chariot of the sun, in a land where houses may not be: I shall love sweetly smiling, sweetly speaking Lalage.

This cannot be expected to sound like poetry, for it was never intended to do so, or to have any of the effects of poetry. One of its most obvious features is its length. Horace's eight lines contain thirty-three words: they illustrate as well as any others the first and perhaps the most characteristic reason for the charm of Horace's verse, his wonderful economy of words. Almost the greatest difficulty that attends the making of a translation of his poetry is the reproduction of the terseness of his style.

The lines illustrate, too, his other great attraction, his

power of constructing a verse in which every word seems to fit exactly into position in the one place to which it inevitably belongs. It is so characteristically Horatian a feature that to try to reproduce it is to learn by experience the significance of Storrs's 'stark impossibility'.

The prose version just given contains fifty-two words. Four other prose versions are sufficiently widely known to invite comparison. They are the translations of:

1. C. E. Bennett (Loeb Library, 1923)
2. J. Lonsdale and S. Lee (Globe Edition, 1882)
3. C. Smart (Bohn Edition, 1850)
4. E. C. Wickham (O.U.P., 1903)

The numbers of words used by these translators are 56, 54, 54 and 66 respectively.

The words which were discussed earlier in this chapter because they seemed to need special attention have been very differently treated by these four writers, and the readiest way of comparing them is in tabular form:

	campis pigris	*recreatur*	*nebulae*	*malusque Iupputer*	*domibus negata*
Bennett	lifeless plains	revives	mists	gloomy sky	denied for dwellings
Lonsdale	plains of lethargy	is fanned	fogs	the malice of the sky	dwellings may not be
Smart	barren plains	is re-freshed	clouds	an inclement atmosphere	deprived of habitations
Wickham	dull plain	wakened to new life	clouds	an inclement Jove	forbidden to human dwelling

To this chart the following comments may be added. The first two writers begin the final couplet, as does Horace, with 'I will love ... ' The others interpose a connective; Smart

says 'there will I love … ' and Wickham 'still shall I love … '
One's feeling is that to omit any connective word tends to
destroy the continuity of the sentiments, but that it should
be the least emphatic word possible, because of its absence
from the Latin. Nothing more than 'and' is needed.

Phrases such as 'plains of lethargy', 'inclement atmosphere', and 'deprived of habitations' are too long and too
polysyllabic to represent Horace well. A more interesting
point is the rendering of the last word, *loquentem*. The obvious
'speaking' seems weak, nor does it go well with 'sweet': and
Bennett and Wickham use 'prattling' and 'prattle'. There is
justification for this. Lalage's name suggests 'La, la', a talka-
tive young woman, or, as she was described at the beginning
of this chapter, a chatterbox. But prattle is not a beautiful
word, and 'chatter' suggests monkeys. Perhaps the choice
between 'sweetly speaking' and 'sweetly prattling' is as
evenly balanced as that between 'homes' and 'houses'.

But whatever is done, a prose translation can scarcely
suggest an ode by Horace, so that the efforts of the versifiers
must be considered.

A version known for many years is that of Roscommon
(1633–85) because it provoked the just criticism of Woodhouselee for so completely changing the sense of the last two
lines. He offered us:

> The burning zone, the frozen isles,
> Shall hear me sing of Celia's smiles;
> All cold, but in her breast, I will despise,
> And dare all heat, but that in Celia's eyes.

The others, and they are many, fall into at least there
groups. First, there are those who, while they do not commit
the enormities of Roscommon, are too far from the atmosphere of Horace to deserve commendation as writers of
acceptable translations. When Edward Marsh (1941) wrote:

Where charioting too near the sultry beach
The sun by noonday shrivels roof and rafter —
Still were I thrall to Lalage's sweet laughter
And sweeter speech.

or when Sir Francis Wrangham (1821) wrote:

Place me where not a roof can rise
So neighbouring Phoebus fires the skies —
Thy cheek of smiles, sweet Lalage,
Thy lip of love my joy shall be.

they have written verse very much of their own making, but
with only an inherited relationship to Horace.

The two remaining groups are divided by their choice of
metre. Horace's metre in this ode was the Sapphic:

first three lines —ᴜ |— — |—ᴜ |ᴜ— |ᴜ—ᴜ
fourth line   —ᴜᴜ |—ᴜ

and there is no obvious reason why this, or something like it,
should not be used in English. On the other hand, the last
group of translators choose a more familiar type of stanza,
and write either in couplets or quatrains. Those who have
adopted the 'English Sapphic', in which the first three lines
of each stanza are rhymed, belong to the school of thought
which hopes that the translation may suggest the original
rhythms; the others are those who are attempting no more
than a poem based on the original: something like it, perhaps,
but recognizably different.

The translators in the former group include A. S. Aylen
(1896), Lord Dunsany (1947), Sir Theodore Martin (1888),
and W. F. Thornton (1878), and it is remarkable that all
these have made considerable departures from the actual
meanings of Horace's words. Thus Aylen's 'An ice-bound
world of mist and snow' pictures a far more wintry scene than
does Horace: Dunsany's 'plateaux' come from the geography,

not the poetry book; and his 'Jove's reviling' is forced on him so that it may be rhymed with 'smiling'; Martin's 'withering tempests freeze from shore to shore' is, again, nothing but the offspring of 'breeze' and 'adore', and Thornton's 'plains where barrenness distresses' is polysyllabic and his 'sable clouds piling' is another of the progeny of 'smiling'.

The writers of rhyming couplets or quatrains include J. Connington (1880), W. H. Cudworth (1917), W. E. Gladstone (1895), and H. B. Mayor (1934). They have faced the same difficulties and in general have suffered the same kind of defeat, but a perusal of their poems suggests another point, whereby they may be compared. One of the obvious features of Horace's last two lines is that Lalage is mentioned by name once, and the adjective *dulce* is used twice. This is something which clearly ought to be retained in the translation, but it is not always to be found. Dr P. Francis does not name her, but calls her 'the nymph', while Connington approaches no nearer than 'that smile ... that voice'. Aylen, Dunsany and Wrangham use 'sweet' or 'sweetly' once each only. Enough has been said to show the nature of the difficulties encountered when this ode is translated into either prose or verse.

Two verse attempts are, however, of outstanding interest; those of W. H. Cudworth and Lord Lytton (1872).

Cudworth's version attracted the attention of Postgate, who pointed out that his adopted metre, three iambic pentameters and one iambic trimeter, gives a total of thirty-six English syllables required to represent the thirty-eight Latin syllables of a Sapphic. Cudworth said that this made the 'superior brevity' of English very obvious, but Postgate disagrees: he says, rightly, that one must never be diffuse in translating Horace, and would equate a Sapphic to twenty-five English syllables only. He does not

show us how this may be done, but Cudworth's last two
lines —

> Yet ever I for Lalage will yearn,
> Sweet-smiling, prattling sweet

— do not give an impression of great compactness.

Lytton's translation makes an ambitious attempt to reproduce the cadences of the classic metre and also abandons
rhyme. His last verse is:

> Place me lone where the earth is denied to man's
>   dwelling,
> All so near to its breast glows the car of the day-god;
> And I still should love Lalage, her the sweet-smiling,
>   Her the sweet-talking.

This is forty-four syllables, and even if one discounts the
superfluous 'lone' in the first line, 'all' in the second, 'And',
'still' and 'her' in the third, and 'her' in the last line, one is
well above Postgate's twenty-five. But taken as a whole it
is an admirable example of a translation which both gives
the sense of the original and keeps continuously before the
reader's mind the fact that it is a rendering of Latin verse.*

The last English translation to be quoted follows the
principle, mentioned in Chapter V, that modern prose-
poetry or poetic prose has a chance of avoiding the disadvantages attaching to both conventional prose and conventional
poetry. It is an interesting and not altogether an unsuccessful
experiment:

> Put me on barren plains
> With no trees reviving in breezes of summer,
> A part of the world by mists
> And a malicious sky oppress'd;

* See Note 5.

Put me below the too-close chariot of the Sun,
In a land for homes unfit,
And sweetly smiling, sweetly chattering
Lalage I shall love.

Evelyn Lambart (1955)

Finally, it must not be forgotten that in our discussion of the translating of Homer we pointed out the possibility of transfusing some of the Homeric spirit into a German translation. Our study of Horace would not be complete if the same device were not attempted here; and in any case it is of interest to see what the writers of other nations have done in the face of the same difficulties.

V. Hundhausen wrote as his last verse:

> *Ich liebe meine Plauderfee*
> *Die wundersüsse Lalage*
> *Und kann den Frohsinn wahren*
> *In Not und in Gefahren.*

This does not give one the impression of being like Horace in style, nor is it at all close to Horace's words. It is, however, short and crisp, and in this respect very different from Gabriel-Gustave de Wailly's rather too lengthy version of 1878:

> *Que sa haine me jette en ces déserts affreux*
> *Du dieu de la lumière inhabitable empire,*
> *Où ses coursiers ardents vomissent tous leurs feux;*
> *Lalage au doux parler, Lalage au doux sourire,*
> *De mon cœur remplira les vœux?*

The conclusion that English translators have little to learn from the French or the Germans would naturally follow from these two examples, but the opinion would be based on slender evidence. Another French translation, made by le Comte de Seignier in 1883 reads:

Mets-moi sur le sol qui semble interdire
Le char du soleil trop bas dirigé :
Partout j'aimerai la voix, le sourire
Si doux ... de Lalage.

These three examples are among the most widely known translations of Horace's poems, but they scarcely encourage further investigations. The truth may be that, while the German language has some advantages for the translation of Homer, the English language is not without advantages for the translation of Horace.

X

Multiple translation

If every man's humour might be followed, there would be no end of translating.

BISHOP BANCROFT

Sir Vincent Massey once wrote, 'Everyone reads, if not always very wisely or very deeply. Almost everyone writes, if not very much or very well.' And to these truths I would add, 'Nearly everyone translates, if not always very happily or very successfully'; and, if the last chapter has not undoubtedly proved this, evidence is to be found in the existence of 168 translations of Pyrrhus.

The gathering together of several or of many attempts to solve the same problems serves to emphasize, as forcefully as possible, one of the characteristics of translation mentioned briefly elsewhere: that there is no one 'correct' translation of any passage of more than a few sentences. Authors do not write with the intention that their words may be readily and accurately translated into other languages; they write for various purposes of their own, after which it sometimes happens that translators fall upon their text and remodel it or ruin it, according to their individual capacities. There is, therefore, no great difficulty in finding a piece of verse or a paragraph of prose which has been translated by several hands, to compare the different versions they have produced, and to determine, when it is possible to do so, the causes of diversity.

To do this is, indeed, a literary exercise which everyone interested in translation will enjoy doing for himself. The compilation of a personal notebook, containing first the original words of the chosen passage, then an abstract of all the notes and comments which different writers have made upon it, then his own translations thereof, literal and literary, and lastly all the translations of it that have been published: all this would form, in fact does form, an experience and, on a small scale, an education in which anyone must delight.

When this is done, or partly done, by someone else, it is bound to lose much of its fascination, because the passage chosen may not appeal to the reader as it did to the writer who chose it; and because the joy of finding, reading and digesting the different versions has disappeared. With this admission that the present chapter must of necessity be subject to considerable discount, an attempt will be made to illustrate the idea.

The choice of the original passage is, of course, an entirely personal or private matter. For our present illustrative purpose the original should clearly be reasonably short, familiar to a large proportion of readers, and above all of sufficient intrinsic merit to have attracted a large enough number of translators to give point to the exercise. Judged by these criteria, a close approach to the ideal would be the famous couplet from *Pervigilium Veneris*, written possibly by Catullus, or possibly by Tiberianus, or equally possibly by someone else:

> *Cras amet, qui nunquam amavit,*
> *Quique amavit cras amet.*

But these lines were quoted, and no fewer than eleven English translations ranging from 1720 to 1956 were collected and discussed, in an admirable recent essay by Mr Oliver Edwards: it would be nothing but an impertinence to plagiarize his opinions in this chapter. The temptation to do so is so great that I compensate myself by recalling a pleasing echo of the rhythm which appeared recently in the cricket columns of a daily newspaper. On the painful topic of the doubtful legality of the bowling of certain gentlemen, a journalist wrote,

> Let him who has always thrown throw on;
> Let him who has never thrown start now.

Delight at finding such an adaptation overcomes dismay at the enormity of the sentiment.

Almost as suitable for our purpose and almost as often translated is the inscription from the column at Sparta. In 480 B.C. Leonidas, King of Sparta, with a thousand men, defended the Pass of Thermopylae, gate to all Greece, against the huge army of Xerxes, King of Persia. The Spartans, faithful to their code of military duty, fought to the death, and a column erected at Sparta to their memory, bore the words:

> Ὦ ξεῖν, ἀγγέλλειν Λακεδαιμονίους ὅτι τῆδε καιμεθα,
> καιμεθα τοις κεινων ῥήμασί πειθόμενοι

Cicero has given us his idea of this tribute as follows:

> *Dic, hospes, Spartae nos te hic vidisse incentis*
> *dum sanctis patriae legibus obsequimur.*

and the English translation which must be given first place because its writer was no less a person than John Ruskin reads:

> O stranger, go and tell our people that we are
> lying here having obeyed their words.

Ruskin wrote this in 'The Crown of Wild Olive' and used straightforward prose which comes very close to a literal translation, a thing that can seldom be done with an approach to success. As close, if not closer, is the rendering of Woodford:

> O stranger, take news to the Lacedemonians that
> here we are lying to their words obedient.

Here, one feels, is an instance in which the simple dignity of the original expressed the unquestioning courage of the fallen and was more closely reproduced by undecorated prose, in direct opposition to the opinion expressed in Chapter VI. There Catullus's 'Odi et amo' undoubtedly called for a verse rendering, so that there can be no surprise that others have cast their translations in the form of a couplet.

W. L. Bowles wrote:

> Go tell the Spartans, thou who passest by,
> That here obedient to their laws we lie.

and Higham and Bourne's version is:

> Take Lacedemonian tidings, passer-by,
> That here, abiding by her word, we lie.

The reader may well enjoy the task of adding his own translation to the five given here, and comparing his result with them.

With the exception of Cicero's translation, the above have all been differing attempts to put the same original into different words in one language. I call this homogeneous multiple translation, in contrast to heterogeneous multiple translation, which is the collection of translations of the same original into different languages. In many ways this is the more interesting study, as was shown by the four versions of 'Lighten our Darkness' earlier in this book.

A worth-while original is, perhaps, not quite so easy to find. If one may judge from such information as is available, the books of today that find their way into the greatest number of European languages are those that describe the unravelling of crimes and the detection of imaginary criminals; and probably a very large collection could be made from translations of the works of Miss Dorothy Sayers and several other writers.

The collection, however, would be of linguistic rather than of literary interest. The most fertile ground must remain with the scriptures, where the field of selection is wide and many translations are reasonably accessible. Almost unapproachable standards have been set by the British and Foreign Bible Society, who published a very popular book containing the words of St John iii, 16 in a quite incredible number of different languages; and also by the Society for the Propagation of Christian Knowledge, who have published translations of our Book of Common Prayer in over two hundred different languages.

Hence at this point a single example should suffice. For anyone who has seen the opening of over ninety terms at Malvern, the choice can scarcely fall anywhere but on the 121st Psalm, and I therefore end this chapter with some versions of its opening verses.

I

Latin
Levavi oculos meos in montes, unde veniet auxilium mihi.
Auxilium meum a Domino, qui fecit caelum et terram.

2

English
I will lift up mine eyes unto the hills, from whence cometh my help;
My help cometh even from the Lord who hath made heaven and earth.

3

French
Je lève mes yeus vers les montagnes,
D'où me viendra le secours?
Le secours me vient de l'Éternel,
Qui a fait les cieux et la terre.

4

German   *Ich hebe meine Augen auf zu den Bergen von welchen mir Hülfe kommt.*
Meine Hülfe kommt vom Herrn, der Himmel und Erde gemacht hat.

5

Spanish   *Alzaré mis ojos a los montes, de donde vendrá mi socorro.*
Mi socorro viene de Jehová, que hizo los cielos y la tierra.

Perhaps the choice was wiser than it seemed. The Hebrew language is unknown to most of us, and is perforce omitted: Latin is not so strange, and the first word of all, *Levavi*, cannot be taken to mean anything but 'I have raised' or 'I have lifted up'. This is not the opening of the familiar English version; and the Jerusalem Bible has:

> I lift my eyes to the mountains,
> Where is help to come from?

This, the most recent reading, seems to follow the ancient Hebrew text, which is generally considered to be most accurately represented by the words:

> I will lift up my eyes to the mountains:
> From whence shall my help come?

The question is asked in order that it may be answered in the second verse; and this is also found in our Revised Version and in the French translation of Osterwald in 1820 and in Segoud's translation of 1873. Almost certainly it is the most acceptable form of words.

This short discussion, raised by a set of four versions of a familiar verse, illustrates very well the surprises which multiple translation can often bring to light, providing one of the many pleasures in the study of the art of translation.

XI

Perfection in translation

The best translators have been those writers who have composed original works of the same species.

WOODHOUSELEE

The belief, widely held by linguists and others, that translation can never be perfect, cannot be accepted without critical thought. It may be true in a general sense that no work of frail man is likely to be without blemish, but in defence of translators as a body of earnest scholars the accusation must at least be examined and, if possible, controverted.

The origin of the myth was made clear in Chapter VI, for it must have sprung from the almost insuperable difficulty of translating poetry. To change the sound of words, as in translating they must inevitably be changed, is also to change their sensuous effect, so that the reader, as inevitably, complains. No one attracted by a verse such as

> Full many a glorious morning have I seen
> Flatter the mountain tops with sovereign eye,
> Kissing with golden face the meadows green,
> Gilding pale streams with heavenly alchemy.

is likely to be comparably moved by

> *Bien des matins j'ai vu la gloire de l'aurore*
> *Caresser les sommets de ses regards royaux,*
> *La face d'or baiser le pré vert qui se dore*
> *Et, céleste alchimiste, empourprer les ruisseaux.*

when this is offered him as an alternative. His disappointment is justified, and the axiom that perfect translation is impossible must be conceded, with the limitation that it is true only of poetry.

And yet, even in writing of the translation of prose, some critics have suggested a standard of excellence which must, frankly, be unapproachable. A perfect translation, it has been said, conveys the spirit of the original author by giving us the words that he would have used had his language been that into which his writings are about to be translated. The finding of these words, it may be added, must take into account the author's style, which depends on his personality as well as the time and the special circumstances in which he wrote.

Not only is this a manifestly impossible demand; it expresses the theory that a translator's function is to transfuse the character of the original author into the translation. This is true only in exceptional circumstances. A translator should concern himself with the words before him; they themselves should sufficiently display their author. What their author wrote is important; how and why he wrote it is only exceptionally of any significance.

Language, however, is not always emotive or affective; often it is symbolic or informative, and the lilt of good prose is not so evanescent as the rhythms of verse. The question may be asked, How, if perfection is approachable, can it be attained, and where are examples of such success to be found?

In answering, or in trying to answer, such questions as these the fallibility of human effort must again be recalled. Perfection must therefore be defined, and in this chapter will be assumed to be attributable to any translation when no critic has been able either to improve upon it or to produce an alternative that is preferred by the majority of readers.

We may brush aside two forms of translation which may be said to deserve the description of perfect. These are, first, the terse public commands or announcements, such as '*Défense de fumer*' where opportunity for error scarcely exists, and, secondly, the translations of industrial, technical or scientific writings, where the factual information to be conveyed is so much more important than anything else that the sounds, associations, and finer shades of meaning of the individual words can be altogether neglected.

Seekers after perfection meet their greatest difficulties in the pages of literature, but where so much has been translated so often and by so many there must be found, if only by the operation of the statistics of chance, examples where, in spite of the long odds, the unexpected has happened. Such examples must be rare, yet one must be sought and presented here, if only to confirm the suggested possibility. A very strong candidate for selection are the six lines of Valéry's *Le Cimitière Marin*:

> *Ils ont fondu dans une absence épaisse,*
> *L'argile rouge a bu la blanche espèce,*
> *Le don de vivre a passé dans les fleurs!*
> *Où sont les morts, les phrases familières,*
> *L'art personnel, les âmes singulières?*
> *La larve file où se forment des pleurs.*

The translation of this into English deservedly won high praise from M. Erik de Mauny: it was written by a poet and so illustrates the principle already mentioned that none but a poet should undertake the translation of poetry. The poet was none other than C. Day Lewis, and he here supplies further evidence that the present is an age of great translators. He wrote:

To an impervious nothingness they're thinned,
For the red clay has swallowed the white kind,
Into the flowers that gift of life has passed.

Where are the dead? — their homely turns of speech,
The personal grace, the soul informing each?
Grubs thread their way where tears were once composed.*

The two thoughts that come to mind when these verses are examined are that such an achievement must have taken considerable learning and much careful thought, and secondly the question, Is there to be found any prescription or advice for approaching this standard by ordinary persons in normal time?

An answer, as satisfactory as any, can luckily be given. Unfortunately, like the solutions to most complex problems, it is in itself complex, for it requires the collaboration of four suitably qualified linguists.

Let these be called A, B, X, and Y; and let the languages involved be, let us say, Welsh and Arabic. A and B are Welshmen who have scholars' knowledge of Arabic, and X and Y are Arabians with equally exact knowledge of Welsh.

In the beginning A and X produce together an Arabian translation of the Welsh original, taking every care to produce a rendering that shall be as good as is possible. Their manuscript is now given to B and Y who, also working together, translate the Arabic back into Welsh. In an ideal world the two Welsh scripts should agree; in practice they will probably not do so. The proportion of divergencies measures the success of the combined operation. In the third stage, all four scholars meet to discuss the discrepancies and to discover their causes so that they can decide whether to make changes in the Arabic translation or not.

When all this has been seriously and competently done, the translation of the Welsh into Arabic can be claimed as perfect, and, if intended for publication, is now ready for the professional critics to tell the experts what they ought to have written.

* From *Collected Poems* (Jonathan Cape and the Hogarth Press, 1954).

XII

Educational translation

'I say, you couldn't help me with my Horace, could you? It was all right for Horace, he could put words in any order he liked, but we have to get them sorted out, and even then they don't make sense. It's that one about the man who is just and tenacious of his proposition, you know the one I mean, but "man" is in the accusative in the very first line, and that isn't English.'

'Horace was not attempting to write English,' said Colin.

ANGELA THIRKELL*

There is no need for more than a superficial acquaintance with the development of education in England to enable one to realize that the art of translation has played an important part therein. The importance has varied, and emphasis has fallen on different languages at different times, but there can be no one who would wish to describe himself as educated, who has not been required, during his struggles to attain the status of scholar, to translate from, and into, at least one language, and probably two or three.

When, in the nineteenth century, the public school system spread throughout the country and established itself as the best form of education for the boys of the time, it inherited the academic side of its work from the old grammar schools. The curriculum was overwhelmingly classical. In a school well known to myself, the Founder laid down the basis of the curriculum in 1597. It included Cicero, Sallust, Caesar, Virgil, Ovid, Horace and Seneca. Nearly three hundred years later a writer, recalling his days at the same school, wrote: 'We did Latin and Greek verses in school and out of school, and (speaking for myself) in bed and in mathematical hours.'

* From *Summer Half* (Hamish Hamilton, 1937).

No one would wish to deny that this kind of education bore an appearance of narrowness; nor could anyone deny that the results, as seen in the achievements of the men who received it, cannot be paralleled by those of later years. It fostered powers of independent thought and produced men of culture and judgment such as are not to be found today, even among electronic engineers or the produce of the comprehensive school.

But before the turn of the century the broadening process had begun. At the school just mentioned, the first master to hold a science degree was appointed in 1894; modern linguists had been in existence for a decade, but the number of boys who took the subjects seriously was not large. Apart from a few freak schools ('where, if a boy does not like mathematics, he is allowed to keep rabbits') this was substantially the position until about the time of the First World War, when the educational experts began to perceive that the rigorous methods of exact scholarship, and the disciplinary training which accompanied it, might be a characteristic of non-classical studies. The scientists had for some time been asserting that they provided a training in clear thinking and accurate practice, and now the professors of modern languages put forward the same claims.

When considered objectively, the opinions of both scientists and linguists seem to be fundamentally sound, for there is not, nor has there ever been, any unarguable reason why a classical education must be considered to be the best education for every child. It may be, and it is, the best type of education for the best brains; but it need not, in consequence, be the best type of education for mediocrity, nor is it.

Arguing along these lines, the modern linguists have, for the past generation and more, taken themselves and their subjects more seriously: they might not unfairly be said to have worked with a greater dignity and with a firmer faith in themselves and in the value of their studies. Boys who have won open scholarships in modern languages at Oxford or Cambridge have no longer been regarded as having unaccountably forsaken the Classical Sixth, but as having wisely redirected their efforts.

Many of those who teach modern languages have been heard to emphasize the fact that translation is only a part of the work and that it is a part that may easily become of an exaggerated importance. They hold that, in the elementary stages of learning, translation is a convenient method of instruction which has the practical advantage that it is easily marked! In the Sixth Forms, however, the maturing scholar should begin to look upon translation as an art, as well as a challenge to his own ability and originality of thought.

The well-known books of R. L. Ritchie and J. M. Moore were among the first and certainly among the most successful expositions of what may be called 'modern scholarship'. Their task was more obvious than easy. They had first to isolate the valuable elements in classical education, apply the principles they had extracted to French (and, by implication, to German, Spanish and Russian), and so to convince their readers that the study of modern languages could be made into as fine an educational instrument as any.

Among many points of great interest, they were able to show that careful study of any language ought to teach the lesson of meticulous accuracy: and any studies which can tend to correct the deplorable and universal sloppiness of thought is to be encouraged. As to the French language itself, they pointed out that the difficulties of translation were different from the difficulties presented by Latin, but that they were just as formidable: and the overcoming of difficulties is a great part of the fundamental purpose of all education. When to these opinions they add their experience that accurate translation from French necessitates literary feeling and a reasonably wide knowledge of English literature, one almost believes that it is a pity that the young should be asked to learn anything else.

The general agreement as to the results of language study provides a pleasant contrast to so much that has been written on the subject of translation. As has already been said, with a somewhat different implication, the person who benefits most from a translation is the translator, and when by much repetition this benefit has continued over a number of years, the accumulated effect on the student's handling of his own language should be very considerable.

There are well-known examples of all kinds to support this opinion. The clearness and precision which are characteristic of the best French prose were found in the English of Lord Macaulay and, much later, in the writing of J. E. Agate and in the German of Heinrich Heine, all of whom were imbued with a love of French. Writers who have clearly absorbed much from a close study of the classics, and who owe much of the character of their own English styles to this, are more numerous. The names of Byron, Gray, Milton, Shelley and Tennyson, for example, are names of five great writers of English who were soaked in classical tradition.

The unquestioned dominance of literary study as a component of a worthwhile education is not difficult to explain. The only significant difference between man and other animals is man's power of abstract thought and rational speech, so that in the making of men the study of the thoughts and words of other men must be of paramount importance. The student of translation must be shown how to answer all three questions which have been recognized as essentials in earlier chapters. What does he say? and the answer involves a knowledge of the difference between *amamus* and *amamur*, between *dirait* and *disait*, between *drucken* and *drücken*. What does he mean? and the answer implies a need to choose between rendering *plume* by 'pen' or 'feather', *porte* by 'door' or 'gate'. How does he say it? and the answer implies an ability to recognize the nature of the writer's style and to reproduce it in a different language.

Taken all in all, this amounts to a very considerable total. It wholly justifies the opinion given throughout this book, that good translation is indeed a laborious business. If it is done as well as possible, it takes a long time.

Language students in their examinations are not, as a rule, offered a very long time in which to make and to write out their translations. They are usually presented with a paper which used to be called 'Unseen', but is now portentously entitled 'Unprepared Translation', containing two or three extracts, one of them in verse, to be translated in an hour and a half or two hours. Now one can take such a passage, glance over it, and produce in fifteen or twenty minutes a rendering which is likely to be 'near enough', or good enough 'to satisfy the examiners'; but one cannot, in the same time, produce a polished version in which one has made the wisest possible choice of every alternative; and one result has been the general comment by examiners that standards of translation are lamentably low.

There can be little doubt that, judged by the standards of Dryden or Postgate, the schoolboy and the undergraduate are likely to produce indifferent versions. Yet in the face of such an admission a reply must be made, first, that the translators are students; they are still learning the language in question; they have not been reading and writing it in the exercise of their profession for a quarter of a century past; and further that they have not yet attained the breadth of acquaintance with English that is needed to enable them to produce the finished translation of the expert.

It would not be reasonable to set the ordinary run of students so short a passage of translation that they would have time to think out a better translation, partly because the examination is not one of translation as such; and partly because the weaker candidates would produce some sort of a result in a very few minutes and nothing that was either different or better, however long they took over the job.

Examiners, therefore, must be content to continue to accept mediocrity in translation; but interesting results would follow from the experiment of setting scholarship and higher candidates a really short passage, and asking them to give a literal, a free and a literary translation, with their own comments on the differences between them. Is there not too much readiness to assume that for a given paragraph of Latin or French there is only one English equivalent, and that the most highly marked candidate must be the one who produces something nearest to this hypothetical ideal? After all, Dr H. M. Butler put Tennyson's 'Crossing the Bar' into twenty-one different sets of Latin and Greek verses.

A very important feature about the educational value of the study of languages depends on the ability of the student to learn at least three languages at the same time. The study of Latin is an admirable training in logical thought for many who do not appreciate the logic in algebra or geometry, but it loses a large part of its value as a study of language if it is the only language being learnt. Today a very large number of boys and girls in secondary schools are being taught French, and a distressingly large proportion of them find it very difficult, or even the most difficult of all the subjects they offer at 'Ordinary Level'. There is little doubt that many of those who find French to be difficult are those who have never learnt any Latin, so that, if my meaning be plain, they come to regard French as a subject and not as a language. The boy or girl who offers French, Latin and German, or French, Latin and Spanish runs no risk of falling into the same error.

I wonder whether it would be possible to create a new examination subject called 'Languages', or, if that were not sufficiently pompous for our examining boards, 'General Linguistics'. I do not know what the objections would be, and no doubt there would be many, but I believe that the experiment would be interesting and perhaps valuable. Certainly it would be no stranger than some of the so-called subjects at present listed in various University Regulations for the G.C.E.

There is an analogy which might justify the attempt. Scientists have for some time past detected the weaknesses in a study of chemistry only or of physics only, and have with increasing success developed a system of teaching and examining in a subject known as General Science. This is intended to form, and when properly operated it does form, either an introduction to further progress in the separate sciences or a necessary part of the mental equipment of a modern citizen who is not a scientist. The proposed General Linguistics might well do for languages what General Science has done for the sciences. It might, in addition, help the scientist to remember, to understand, and even to spell the words in which his science is written; it might silence the critic who says that a boy may have learnt French or German for four years and yet be unable to read or to speak either language; it might even be so constructed that it would stimulate an ability to think. At present the University of London allows candidates for the General Certificate of Education to choose from among fifty-eight languages at Ordinary Level and thirty-seven at Advanced and Scholarship or Special Level. There should be material here for a subject of sufficient breadth.

The following may yet be read in the Regulations issued by the University of Gondwanaland in '1984'.

LANGUAGES

Ordinary Level. There will be one paper of three hours. Candidates may offer English with not less than three and not more than five other languages named in any section of the Approved List given below.

Advanced Level. There will be two papers of three hours each. Candidates may offer English with not less than three and not more than five other languages which must be taken from at least two groups in the Approved List.

Special Paper. There will be one paper of three hours. Candidates will be given opportunities to display either (i) knowledge of languages other than those chosen for their Advanced Level papers, or (ii) knowledge of foreign literature, or (iii) ability to conduct a conversation and practise interpretation in one chosen language.

LIST OF APPROVED LANGUAGES

Group 1. Anglo-Saxon, Gaelic, Welsh, Erse, Manx, Cornish.

Group 2. Latin, Italian, French, Spanish, Portuguese.

Group 3. Greek, German, Dutch, Russian, Polish or Finnish, Norwegian or Swedish.

Group 4. Afrikaans, Arabic, Persian, Yoruba, Hindi, Urdu, Malay, Siamese.

With the first announcement of this innovation, a Specimen Paper will no doubt be issued.

LANGUAGES
Ordinary Level
Time allowed, three hours

Answer any five questions

1. Four great alphabets are Hebrew, Greek, Roman and Cyrillic; discuss the differences between them.

2. Compare the effects of declension, word-order, and the use of prepositions as alternative means of expression.

3. Translate the following sentences three times, using three of your selected languages once each:

    (*a*) He carefully read the letter which his friend had written.

    (*b*) When he had finished he took his pen and began to write a reply.

    (*c*) Although he was angry he wrote slowly, but made his answer short and ...

    Supply the last word yourself.

4. Compose a paragraph of from four to eight lines in a language other than English, and then rewrite it in any other language, excluding English.

5. Write in tabular form, i.e. in vertical columns, the names of

    (i) The days of the week,

    (ii) The months of the year,

    (iii) The numerals from one to ten,

    in each of your three languages.

6. The following words are all applied to the same animal: *arachne, araneus, araignée, spider, Spinne, Arana, Ragno, Spin, Edderkop, precoppin, pajakov.* Comment on and as far as possible explain their similarities and differences.

7. Write a short essay in a language other than English on one of the following subjects:

Shakespeare	Dogs
Travel	Money

XIII

Pseudo-translation

If you really thought the original was like that, what can you have seen in it to make you think it was worth translating?

ROBERT BRIDGES

There is often something to be learnt from a comparison between the length of a translation and the length of its original. A difference may be due in part to the structural character of the languages, as when the three Latin words *Ex urbe condita* must be rendered by the six English words 'From the foundation of the city', or conversely when seven French words '*C'est moi qui l'a fait*' are equated to three English words 'I did it'. Alternatively, it may be due to the difference in the literary styles of the translator and the original author. This is shown when several translations of the same original are quantitatively compared. The first book of the *Aeneid* occupies 756 lines and Billson's translation of it is also 756 lines in length. James Rhoades needed 947 lines and Dryden 1,065. This last figure represents a 41 per cent increase, a fact which, in itself, must have a noticeable effect on the character of the result.

An unequalled example of expansion in translation is to be found in Tate and Brady's version of Psalm 34. The Prayer Book reads 'I will always give thanks unto the Lord', where the adverb is a translation of the Vulgate's one word, *semper*. In Hymn 290 this becomes

> Through all the changing scenes of life,
> In trouble and in joy,

or twelve words for one.

So extreme an increase may be condoned by saying that the hymn was never intended to be a translation, but to be an adaptation or, as is familiar in Scotland, a rhymed version, or, in one word, a paraphrase. As soon as faithfulness in translation is abandoned in favour of unlimited freedom a translation tends to become a paraphrase; and one of the normal features of any paraphrase is that it is longer than its original. In prose this is of no great consequence; in poetry, where the quantity, the mere number of words, is a part of the nature of the poem, the importance is far greater.

Thus arises the question, When is a translation not a translation? and the answer is, When it is a new version or a new rendering; and the reason for the question is that the composer of any such paraphrase may not have read the original nor even have been able to do so.

Manifestly, anyone can choose any page, passage or paragraph that for any reason attracts him, and, reading and re-reading it for the pleasure that such repetition produces, come at the last to find flaws in its perfection. To try to remove them is vital to his peace of mind, and straightway he sets himself the task of rewriting or editing and trying to improve the jewel that once had seemed beyond compare. Let an example be given.

Many years ago a young man in love came, almost by chance, upon the 'Song of Songs' and found there a reflection of his own temporary state of mind. But as it is printed in the Authorized Version its beauty is all but obliterated. The artificial verses, the double columns, the unannounced changes of speaker, the marginal notes might almost have been designed to prevent the reader from gaining a true appreciation of one of the greatest love poems in literature. It was a labour of love indeed to rewrite the whole Song so as to display its semi-dramatic nature, and the result was delightful to read. It seemed, at least to its maker, to be an improvement on the obscure original, but it was a revision of the Song that owed nothing to earnest study of ancient manuscripts. It was not a work that any publisher would consider:* it was a transcript, an adaptation, but not a translation.

The conclusion begins to emerge that in certain, more extreme cases a translation is not representative of its original in any but the primitive sense of a transcript of its meaning: it is a new product and perhaps an incentive to a study of the original.

Obviously, this applies most freely to the translation of poetry. A poem, which derives its name from ποιέω, to make, is a thing made, and if it is made of English words it is a different thing from a poem made of French or Spanish words, just as inevitably as a house made of bricks is different from a house built of stone.

Accepting the inevitable, some translators have carried freedom to the limit; others have passed it and turned freedom into licence. A very good illustration of the former is provided by the ever-popular *Rubáiyát* of Omar Khayyám, as translated by Edward Fitzgerald.

Since that poem is of considerable length, one stanza only will be used, and I have chosen one that seems well suited to a baffled scientist and therefore likely to appeal to most readers in a scientific age:

> Myself when young did eagerly frequent
> Doctor and saint, and heard great argument
>   About it and about, but evermore
> Came out by the same door as in I went.

A word-for-word translation of the original Persian reads something like this:

* The Folio Society in fact issued *The Song of Songs* in May 1967.

For a while in childhood we attended a master;
for a while we were happy with our own mastery;
at the end of the story see what happened to us —
like water we entered, and like wind we departed.

This version is given by Dr A. J. Arberry in his treatise on the poem.

Two other renderings may here be quoted, with the confession that I have been unable to ascertain whether they were made by consultation with the Persian or with any other translation:

J'avais un maître alors que j'étais un enfant,
Puis je devins un maître et par là triomphant;
Mais écoute la fin: tout cela en somme
Un amas de poussière emporté par le vent.

Zum Meister ging ich einst — das nur die Jugendzeit —
Dann hab' ich mich der eigenen Meisterschaft gefreut,
Und wollt ihr wissen, was davon das Ende ist?
Den Staubgeborenen hat wie Staub der Wind zerstreut.

A moment's comparison of these stanzas shows that to their separate authors the words and sentiments of Omar were used in large part as suggestions for emotions that they wished to express in their own ways. Their actions may be condoned because they have written acceptable verses which have been read by many and have given them the pleasure that the reading of verse brings, but a linguist must point out that they have carried the principle of freedom to its limits.

The limit, however, can be overstepped, and then the product can scarcely be called a translation by any charitable means. An example is to be found in the lines of Catullus,

Soles occidere et redire possunt
Nobis, cum semel occidit brevis lux,
Nox est perpetua una dormienda.

for which Sir Walter Raleigh offered:

The sun may set and rise
But we contrariwise
Sleep after our short light
One everlasting night.

In a comment on this 'sorry jingle' a writer in the Press some years ago produced a wonderfully ironic example of how not to do it, to show how great a difference it is possible to create between a line or two of poetry and its carefree English rendering. He chose

Atque in perpetuum, frater, ave atque vale.

and, with sacrilege aforethought, printed:

Buddy
So long
From now
On.

I wonder if translators have ever thought of organizing a competition the object of which was to reproduce the meaning of a given model while at the same time departing as far as possible from its style and atmosphere. If such a contest were to be held I feel that a high place would be gained by Dr Whitehead's interpretation of the series:

Cogitatio, imaginatio, delectatio, assensio.

For this the readers of the *Sunday Times* were offered, 'I muse and then let my imagination get to work until I delight in some sensual scene and finally I fall.' Could there be a finer example of a 'translation' that so completely neglects the genius of a language? Four incisive abstract nouns that bring their own rhythms to the line are here presented as a verbose, ill-expressed, and scarcely exact statement which is not what the original writer said and is not cast in the way in which he said it.

One can imagine a comparable version of Julius Caesar's famous

Veni, vidi, vici.

which might by Dr Whitehead's method become, 'I reached the country after long marches, I surveyed the position before undertaking military action, and in this I successfully subjugated the defenders.'

I end this short chapter by giving the most typical, or perhaps the most exaggerated, example of pseudo-translation that can easily be found. There is a sentence well known to users of typewriters: 'The quick brown fox jumps over the lazy dog', and anyone unaccustomed to these machines might well be misled into translating this by: *Le rapide renard brun saute au-dessus du chien paresseux*, whereas the sophisticated stenographer might well know that the usual French equivalent is: *Zoe, ma grande fille, veut que je boive ce whisky dont je ne veux pas.*

One may note in passing that whereas the English language succeeds in using all the letters of the alphabet in nine words, the French language takes fifteen, and that the last five words are needed for only four letters.

I have been unable to discover an equivalent sentence in use in Germany, though there may well be one that has eluded me. This may stimulate others to construct a German version, or, for that matter, Latin, Spanish, Greek and Italian ones as well.

XIV

Science in translation

*Although a scientist is seldom hailed as a scholar, he is always supposed
to be able to read the latest work on his own speciality, whether it has
been published in French or German, Norwegian or Russian.*
THE LANGUAGE OF SCIENCE

The words quoted above suggest that translations of scientific
books are made and published less often than are translations
of any other kind. The fundamental principles of science,
which are based on knowledge of material events, have
always been freely interchanged among men of all nations,
until of late the progress of civilization has made them hesitate to share their knowledge of the fission of the atom.
Therefore the data needed to write a scientific book have
always been available in the country and in the language of
an author, who has naturally availed himself of them. He
has written his book for his own countrymen, while a few
scores or a few hundreds of miles away another scientific
author is writing a very similar book on the same or nearly
the same subject, in another language for another set of
readers.

Both authors, who have possibly corresponded with each
other for years, are helped by the fact that science specialists,
who alone are concerned with the most recent discoveries
and the most novel ideas, normally obtain their information
not from books but from papers published in scientific
journals. The custom of all journals of repute is to supply
each contributor with a number of reprints of his paper,
which he distributes to his co-workers interested in the
subject. In consequence the linguistic obstacle that faces the

scientist is no more than a matter of ten, twenty, or perhaps sixty pages, and the task of digesting such a relatively small amount is a very different matter from the labour of struggling through a whole volume. Moreover, a paper printed in one of the less familiar languages is often accompanied by a summary in English, French or German, and many a scientist is content gratefully to make do with no more, or with very little more, than this.

Why, therefore, it may be asked, if the optimism of this page be justified, is the subject of science in translation deemed to be worthy of a chapter to itself? There are four reasons.

First, translations of scientific works, even though they do not compare in extent with translations of literature, none the less occupy a reasonable corner of the translators' field, and a corner which, so far from being negligible, is of rapidly increasing importance. In a scientific world the spreading of scientific knowledge must take a prominent place and must occupy the attention of a number of scientific authors. A book which aims at being a survey of translations of all kinds is therefore obliged to give adequate attention to science.

Secondly, the translation of scientific work is an ideal example of translation in writing in which the subject-matter is wholly in the ascendant and the style is scarcely considered. It forms, perhaps, the extreme term in a series in which the relative values of matter and manner vary inversely with one another, until, as in a Horatian lyric, the manner far surpasses the matter.

Thirdly, the translation of scientific work illustrates extremely well the necessity for some knowledge on the part of the translator of the subject about which the original was written: and fourthly, there are features about the words of science which are so characteristic that they give an aspect to scientific translation that can scarcely be found elsewhere.

This is no place to discuss the position of science in modern life nor the value of scientific knowledge in modern living: these things become increasingly obvious year by year, almost month by month. They have but little to do with the work of translation, and the first of the four reasons just mentioned may therefore be passed by with no further considerations: the others demand our attention.

The content of a scientific book is founded on facts, discovered by observation and experiment, discussed in terms of hypotheses, and tested by further experiments. Its reader is concerned to learn these facts, follow the experiments, and appreciate the hypotheses; he is seldom, if ever, concerned with the literary style of the author. This is to say that, although he may find his reading the easier for a clear exposition, or perhaps more often the harder for an involved manner of expression, he does not read a scientific book for the sensuous pleasure it gives. An intellectual pleasure he may well receive, but this is an enjoyment of a different genre from the pleasure of reading Ruskin or Swinburne. In consequence, a scientific book is seldom read because of the attractiveness of the author's style: style is something that the scientific writer is only too prone to leave to look after itself, with results that are not always commendable. One much discussed feature of a translator's work thus disappears; or perhaps it assumes a different form. He is quite free from any demand that his translation shall reflect the literary quality and the measured rhythms of his author: he may well be expected to improve the work in this respect. It was Dr Johnson who said, 'A translator is to be like his author: it is not his business to excel him.' Dr Johnson can have had but little idea of the dreadful jargon which scientists of later days were going to compose.

There are, of course, exceptions, and probably every scientist who has read at all widely can recall instances that he has met. In this country the biological writings of Professor D'Arcy Thompson have always been noted for their literary grace. I myself retain a memory of reading Moissan's *Le Fluor*, which a wise schoolmaster had put into my hands, and of enjoying the terse clearness of his beautiful French prose quite as much as the fascination of his story of the successful isolation of fluorine. Again, Dr Wilhelm Filchner's *Zum Sechsten Erdteil* records the scientific results of his expedition in 1911 to the head of the Weddell Sea, in clear German prose which by itself makes the reading of the book a pleasure. Books of this kind scarcely need to be translated.

The writer of science, whether he pays attention to literary style or whether he leaves it to chance, must always keep an alternative ideal in the front of his mind. This ideal is clearness of exposition. Scientific books are studied for the information they contain, and their readers include those who already know their subjects more or less thoroughly, those who are more familiar with other branches of science, and others, perhaps in smaller proportion, who know but little science. Because all these are seeking information, the principle of 'reader-analysis', useful in other chapters of this book, is here made sterile. All readers want the same lucidity of expression; and in addition to verbal accuracy this, and this only, is the ideal that the translator must set before himself. All those commentaries on translation which have asserted that a translation should have all the ease of original composition, that it should give no clue to the language from which it was translated, or that comparison between the original and the translation should provide no evidence as to which was which, should be accepted without hesitation as being wholly applicable to the translation of science.

This apotheosis of clearness precludes all the emotional content of a sentence which is derived from the associations which its words carry. Scientific words do not accumulate the associations and implications of ordinary words, and with this there disappears the whole of what may approach or become eloquence in an ordinary paragraph.

That there is no emotion and no eloquence in scientific writing is not a consequence of the nature of the scientist, but derives from a tradition which dates back to the seventeenth century. From its foundation the Royal Society determined to reject 'all the Amplifications, Digressions and Swellings of Style', and enjoined upon its members a 'close, naked, natural way of speaking'. This is the explanation of the outstanding characteristic of scientific writing, which makes its translation so much more direct, so much freer from alternatives, so much less artistic than the translation of any other kind of prose.

The translation of works of science illustrates better than any other kind the advantages that follow if the translator has some knowledge of the subject under discussion, but this does not mean that by compensation an adequate knowledge of the translated language is not as necessary as elsewhere. Two instances may be quoted in illustration.

In 1958 General de Gaulle found it necessary to introduce a degree of austerity into the French Budget, and was reported in the B.B.C.'s News Bulletin to have announced increased taxes on 'wine, alcohol and tobacco'. This appears to imply that French wine contains no alcohol. Evidently the words *vin, alcool et tabac* had been translated as above, where the correct rendering should have been 'wine, spirits and tobacco'.

The memory of an otherwise insignificant experience may also be recalled. Some years ago, after the completion of a translation of Kostitzin's *Biologie Mathématique*, I took a copy of the newly published book to the Science Library of my school. Three of my good friends were there. 'What,' asked one of them, 'do you know of French?' 'And what,' added another, 'do you know of mathematics?' 'Or what,' capped the third, 'do you know of biology?' It is to be observed that of the three spontaneous questions one only was concerned with knowledge of the language, and two were concerned with knowledge of the subject-matter.

The influence on translation of the character of the words of science is of great importance. Apart from a few words, which the scientists have borrowed from ordinary speech, and used with meanings of their own ('force' and 'work' are obvious examples), the words of science are inventions, made each for a specific purpose. The result is that each scientific word has one meaning and one meaning only, precisely defined on the occasion of its first appearance, and unlikely to change thereafter. This is in sharp contrast to such words as 'box' or 'train', to name two examples of familiar words each of which has a number of completely different meanings. Further, scientific words are more often than not the same, or nearly the same, in all languages, and do not call for translation. The words of science have been compared to the symbols of mathematics, and in fact they are often as universally intelligible as is the statement that $(a + b)^2 = a^2 + 2ab + b^2$, whether it occurs in a Polish or a Portuguese algebra book.

The consequence of these features of scientific translation are clear enough: a translation of a scientific work may deserve to be described as a perfect translation in a sense that few literary translations can match. It remains only to add a couple of features of scientific translation which further define its character. The first is the simple one that just as most scientific works are written, so also are scientific translations made, for scientists to read. The scientific vocabulary is now so specialized that only a scientist can find a continuing interest in reading science; for other readers it approaches too closely to the unintelligible. And the second is that a scientific translation is almost always made from a recent original work, to be read by its contemporaries. Both these factors help to separate scientific translations from translations of all other kinds.

The foregoing commentary demands something in the way of an example which will illustrate the points that have been made. The following passage occurs in Alfred Wegener's *Neuere Forschungen auf dem Gebiete der atmosphärischen Physik*:

> *Noch ein andere Erscheinung spielt eine ausserordentlich grosse Rolle bei den Formen der Wolken. Dies sind der Fallstreifen. Der Niederschlag, der sich in der Wolke bildet, sinkt ja vermöge seiner Schwere herab, verdampft aber in den meisten Fällen sogleich wieder, sobald er die untere Grenze der Wolke erreicht hat und in die ungesättigte Luft hineinsinkt. Wenn er aber schon gröbere Formen angenommen hat, oder namentlich, wenn er aus Schnee oder Eis besteht und daher nicht so schnell verdunsten kann, so sinkt er noch mehr oder weniger weit in die tieferen Schichten hinab, ehe er sich ganz auflöst. In den Fällen, wo er den Erdboden erreicht, sprechen wir von Regen oder Schnee.*

Yet another phenomenon plays an unusually large part among cloud-forms. This is the 'mare's tail'. The precipitation that forms in a cloud sinks by reason of its weight, but in most cases it evaporates again as soon as it reaches the lower surface of the cloud and enters unsaturated air. But if it has already assumed a more substantial form, and especially if it consists of snow or ice and thus cannot diffuse so rapidly, it falls more or less deeply to lower levels before it disappears altogether. In some cases it reaches the ground, and we call it rain or snow.

This extract was taken from a German book because among languages other than English German has for long held a prominent place in science. Ambitious young scientists have often been encouraged to learn German, just as they are today being encouraged to learn Russian, because such knowledge would be a real practical help to them in their careers. But because German is often an easier language to translate than French, a paragraph of French science should be added, to supplement the German and to confirm the opinions expressed in this chapter.

In that fascinating and imaginative book, *La Vieillissement du Monde Vivant* by Henri Decugis, a book which surprisingly has never received in this country the appreciation that it unquestionably deserves, we may read the following:

> *L'écorce terrestre est, en réalité, un immense cimitière de végétaux et d'animaux appartenant à des familles disparues, ou n'ayant laissé que de rares survivants. Sans doute, la filiation est indéniable. L'arbre généalogique des êtres organisés a été constamment en se ramifiant et en se diversifiant, ce qui laisserait même supposer l'existence actuelle de formes de plus en plus nombreuses. Il faut bien constater cependant qu'il n'en est rien. La plupart de ces rameaux sont morts depuis fort longtemps. Ceux qui subsistent n'ont plus que les représentants sensiblement moins nombreux. Les exemples de ces extinctions abondent.*

The earth's crust is actually an immense graveyard of plants and animals belonging to families which are either extinct or which are represented by a few survivors only. The connection is certainly undeniable. The genealogical tree of living organisms has changed and branched so often that one is led to imagine the existence today of more and more numerous species. But there is nothing of the kind. Most of the branches are long since dead; those that survive have appreciably fewer representatives. Examples of such extinctions abound.

It appears from an examination of these four passages that

scientific writing has little or nothing to lose by being translated. The extracts support and confirm the contention that not only is it possible, but that it is not even very difficult, to produce a perfectly satisfactory transcript of a page of science; perfect, that is to say, in that it fulfils all the requirements of a translation that have been put forward by the experts. As a consequence there is an unimportant feature of scientific translation which provides a significant conclusion to this section. A scientific work does not get translated twice into the same language. Whereas the translations of the *Aeneid* or the *Divine Comedy* are almost beyond the counting, there is no example known to me of alternative translations of any scientific book.

XV

Translation in industry

Good translations are one of the vital necessities of our time.
F. L. LUCAS

There may be bought today a piece of red cloth so treated that if it is used to wipe a sheet of glass, water vapour will not readily condense on its surface. This miracle, a boon to the motorist who wishes for a clear windscreen, is sold in a plastic bag on which 'Instructions for Use' are printed in six languages. To supplement this there may be quoted a recent invitation to visit 'One of the world's most important exhibitions exclusively for those who control and operate laboratories of every type' where turning a page, I read a similar appeal to *'ceux qui organisent et dirigent les laboratoires de toutes sortes'*; to *'die, denen die Leitung und der Betrieb von Laboratorien aller Art anvertraut sind'*; to *'coloro che dirigono e gestiscono laboratori di ogni genere'*; and to *'los que dirigen y operan laboratorios sea cual sea su tipo'*.

These two simple examples are such as any reader is likely to have met, and they give an admirable proof of the way in which the nations of the world are becoming more closely knit while at the same time they are meeting the handicap of their different languages. Whether the industrialists are addressing the ubiquitous motorists or the practising scientists, they have found that successful publicity may involve manifold translations of their messages.

Thus there is introduced the need for translation, and incidentally for the employment of translators, in the world of commerce, industry and technology; and this opens a wide field which leads directly to comparable needs and uses for translation in diplomatic, judicial, naval and military circles. All this covers a vast amount of translating and an equivalent amount of intellectual work, which is necessary to keep our complex civilization going as it should. It is also the best proof of the fact, already mentioned, that the nations pay a high price for the privilege of using their own languages.

A few characteristics of this kind of translation must be mentioned.

First, and most obviously, it is almost entirely a practical, unemotional exercise. Facts, opinions, arguments are its materials, to be stated with a clarity and emphasis that will carry conviction rather than with a literary eloquence that will give intellectual pleasure. This does not mean careless or carefree translating, for few processes are more subtle than the persuading of other men to spend their money on goods of whose value they are perhaps uncertain. Several established and recognized writers who have on occasions turned their hands to this kind of pot-boiling have left evidence of the seemingly disproportionate amount of thought that they gave to the work to ensure a successful result.

Secondly, while in general the demands on the translator are no less serious than those that have been met already, there are special instances where the difficulties are quite as insuperable. To call a spade a spade is believed, proverbially, to be an ideally direct process, but an experienced and careful translator would be unlikely to agree with this. He would know that in parts of Europe and South America the word 'spade' suggests a 'hoe', and the word 'hoe' suggests a shovel. Hence a spade should not be called a *bêche* but a *pelle*, and a *bêche* should be called a *houe*, the whole forming an absurd tangle of local names and customs.

Or again, if a cinema film is to be adapted for exhibition in another country, the sound track carrying the spoken words of the characters will need to be replaced. But the newer words will be such as are associated with different movements of the lips, and to an attentive audience the disparity may become too obvious. How, asks Mr Cary in discussing this matter, can a man who is seen to be saying *Oui, mon capitaine* and is heard to be saying 'Yes, Sir' fail to produce a feeling that something has gone awry? And finally, only one who is familiar with French practice is likely to realize that *ciment* may have to stand for 'concrete' as well as for 'cement'.

The terminology of the engineers and other technicians is surprisingly copious. Even a comparatively simple machine may be composed of dozens or scores of separate parts, and even in different districts of the same country these may not (in fact almost certainly will not) be known by the same names. Hence a description of a vacuum pump translated into Italian may be appreciated in Brindisi and may be far less intelligible in Genoa. The British Standards Bureau makes efforts to reduce this kind of ambiguity. In 1955 one of its recommendations advised a reduction of six thousand names of varied occupations in British coalmining to three hundred, a fact which shows that translation into English of a foreign text dealing with these duties would have nineteen chances in twenty of being misunderstood each time that one of them was mentioned.

The good technical translator foresees this kind of imperfection in his work, and his readers should be able to trust his judgment in overcoming it. Differences in technical procedure may make a sentence which is quite clear to those who read it in their own language hopelessly obscure to others who read it literally and accurately translated. Hence the translator is compelled to tackle the job of making his translation 'better than the original'. We have met this idea before and have dismissed it briefly as being of small consequence in literary translation. In industry and technology it may be absolutely essential.

Clearly, therefore, the technical translator requires no less ability than does the translator of Homer, and, in addition to linguistic knowledge and experience in the art of translation, he needs more than a superficial knowledge of the subject. Obviously a translator so qualified will command a high salary, or otherwise he will use his ability elsewhere. Thus technical translations are expensive. Dr Holmstrom has pointed out that a journal or a report may cost a technologist perhaps 2s. and the making of a translation thereof may cost £10. Hence he has to decide whether the original, which he cannot be sure of reading with understanding, is going to be worth a hundred times as much when it is translated. The world of the technician is a hard one in this respect, and may still deserve much of the harrowing description written by Dr L. L. Sell in 1945:

The desperate patent attorney, vainly seeking some non-existent authoritative dictionary to find the proper Spanish or Portuguese terms of a new patent, to prevent the sneers of a critical client; the despondent translator, groping his way with the technical terms of a catalogue which is to be printed in some foreign language, on which his reputation and his livelihood usually depend − all but too often lost as a result of his pains; the nervous clerk who had picked the wrong meaning from a poor polyglot technical dictionary and now faces the unsavoury task of explaining to his employer the reason for a shipment which the customer did not order; the deflated foreign language 'expert', upon whose faulty judgments, seconded by an equally faulty technical dictionary, an official has submitted a report based on false information; these constitute only a few of the many examples of the great army of miserables, trudging

their uncomfortable ways along the bumpy thorough-
fares of international relations.*

In so machine-minded a generation as the present the
possibility that the work of translation could be in part per-
formed by a machine must often have occured to the minds of
writers. The first record of the realization of this dream appears
to have been made in 1939 when a Russian pioneer P. P.
Smirnov Troyansky claimed to have invented such a machine.

Progress, however, was negligible until the computer made
its now considerable impact on modern life, and Dr Andrew
Booth suggested to William Warren of the Rockefeller Foundation that computers might help translators. Dr Booth has said
that his suggestion was merely 'an intellectual exercise',
attempting to find further uses for these new machines. Dr
Warren responded and soon published a memorandum on
the subject of 'Translation'. Thus the scheme took shape.

In 1954 there was held in New York a demonstration of
machine-translating, one of the first of its kind. The '701'
general purposes computer of the International Business
Machines Company was used; it was programmed with a
vocabulary of 250 words and six rules of syntax, and it made an
encouraging attempt to translate Russian into English. Three
years later the Cambridge Language Research Unit perfected
plans for a machine which would translate one language not
into one other but into any other language. Little more has
been heard of this ambitious project, whereas by 1960 it was
reported that an American computer was daily making translations from *Pravda* into 'primitive but intelligible English'. Its
vocabulary numbered several tens of thousands of words and
its rate of working was several dozens of words a minute.

Thus within little more than a decade the situation for
computer translating seemed to be a favourable one. There

* From Scientific and Technical Translation (UNESCO, 1957).

were difficulties, inevitably, but to the technicians concerned these appeared as merely temporary obstacles. Yet, by 1961, when an international conference was held at Teddington, belief in mechanical translating had clearly declined, and no arresting of this decline was obvious at the 1965 Conference on Computational Linguistics held in New York. Prevailing opinion today would probably maintain that computers cannot do the work of translating as usefully or as effectively as professional translators, and that the attempt to replace human effort by the machine has failed. The reason for this rather surprising belief should be considered.

The limitations of mechanical translation arise, first and most obviously, from the aesthetic nature of translating, a characteristic which this book has striven to emphasize. An almost fundamental feature of a machine is the constancy of its reaction to one and the same stimulus, the consequence of which appears to be that any word offered, supplied or 'fed into' the translating computer must always produce the same word in translation. As has been seen, a real translation is not made in this way.

In the second place, the nature of a computer must be remembered. Because popularly written descriptions spoke of the computer's storage capacity as its memory there was a general tendency to regard the computer as a kind of robot brain, which could function better than the mind of man and could even create conceptions by its own automatic activity. This is not so: a computer has no background of knowledge and experience; it is no more than an efficient and, particularly, a rapidly working tool, which can work in the service of the human intellect to which it owes its existence.

This important limiting factor was evident from the first, when the early translations were described as crosses between Babu and Basic. An example, given by Dr J. E. Holmstrom in 1954, will illustrate this:

First, the original text, to which the pre-editor has added vertical lines at 'loci of decomposition': these mark off the endings that denote plurals and tenses:

Il n'est pas étonn | ant de constat | er que les hormone | s de croissance ag | issent sur certain | es espèce | s, alors qu'elles sont in | opér | antes sur d'autre | s, si l'on song | e à la grand | e spécificité de ces substance | s.

Secondly, the mechanical translation:

v not is not step astonish *v* of establish *v* that/which? *v* hormone *m* of growth act *m* on certain *m* species *m*, then that/which? *v* not operate *m* on the other *m* if *v* one dream/consider *z* to *v* great *v* specificity of those substance *m*.

Here the interpolated symbols have the following significance to the post-editor:

$$v = \text{vacuous or meaningless}$$
$$m = \text{dual or plural}$$
$$z = \text{unspecific}$$

From this the post-editor, a specialist in the subject-matter but not in the original language, produces the final version:

It is not surprising to learn that growth hormones may act on certain species while having no effect on others, when one remembers the narrow specificity of these substances.

As this extract suggests, mechanical translation has been reasonably helpful in scientific or technical work, and obviously this is because in any one branch of science there are about a thousand words that specially belong to it, and at the same time the equivalent of each in another language is invariable. The German *Sauerstoff* is always to be translated by 'oxygen', and neither literary ability nor aesthetic sense can alter the fact. To the thousand scientific words another thousand words in general use may be added, and the total forms a limited micro-glossary, as it is called, well within the capacity of the computer. The programming of the machine *is* then determined by the particular micro-glossary in use, and will depend on the actual science that it is translating.

This example also illustrates the fundamental fact about computer-translating, namely that the machine must be fed with data prepared by a pre-editor, and this is not always a simple process. It is, in fact, a technique of its own, studied by those who wish to become computer-operatives. Mr Edmond Cary has given a striking illustration of this, from one point of view. He points out that so expensive a device as a computer can be used profitably only if it is working continuously, which means that it must be fed with perforated tape at the rate of two million characters a minute. Since a programmer cannot make more than 10,000 characters an hour one minute of the machine's work involves 200 hours or 12,000 minutes of programming; or, to put it another way, 12,000 secretaries are necessary to feed the computer 'economically'.

And even this assumes that the programming is simple and straightforward, which it may not be. By some complex devices a computer must be made able to distinguish such remarks as 'I am training for a race' and 'For a train I am racing'. It must also be enabled to take account of the different structures of the different languages: indeed, it has been said that the greatest benefit that has come from the computer-translator has been the stimulus it has given to semantic research Until more investigation has been devoted to these problems, the position is one that is almost unique in technology, for who would have foreseen that, when the computer was put to this operation, the greatest difficulty would be found in telling it what to do?

XVI

Translators' humour

I don't know how, cheerfulness was always breaking in.
MR EDWARDS to DR JOHNSON

There is no aspect of man's activity in which there can be found no place for humour, no cause for laughter: if it were not so, life would be uninspiring in youth and intolerable in old age. And if any sober-minded kill-joy would voice the contrary opinion let him be reminded that of a truly solemn occasion we read: '*Σὺ εἶ πέτρος, καὶ ἐπὶ ταύτῃ τῇ πέτρα οἰκοδομήσω μου τὴν ἐκκλησίαν.*' 'Thou art Peter, and upon this rock I will build my church.' (Matt. xvi, 18.) Unhappily, the pun on which the Christian Church was founded is lost in translation into English, though it survives in Latin.

Humour, therefore, must be expected to enter into translation, and in fact it makes its appearance very early in the student's experience, or perhaps more accurately in his inexperience, when his attempts to translate produce surprising or ludicrous results.

Howlers, as they are traditionally termed, are common enough in the lives of all teachers; they have several times been collected and published, and sometimes criticized as spurious inventions because they have seemed too good to be true. Writing as one who has collected scientific howlers for over forty years, I can assure the sceptics that the rate of supply is sufficient to make forgery unnecessary.

There are, however, degrees of absurdity among howlers of all kinds. A mere mistake does not make the grade; the essence of a howler is that the clue to the misapprehension should be reasonably obvious, that is to say the translation offered must be a translation of other words which resemble or suggest the words that are actually printed. Because *l'habile ouvrier* looks to the unobservant like *l'habit ouvert* it becomes a howler when, instead of 'the clever workman' it is translated as 'with his coat unbuttoned'. Any jest, however, loses all its appeal when it is analysed in this way.

The number of first-class linguistic howlers is so great that some self-discipline must be imposed in quoting samples. Since the two most important languages in schools are Latin and French, ten specimens are divided between them:

From Latin:
  i. *Caerulae puppes:* Skye terriers.
  ii. *Cave canem:* beware! I may sing.
  iii. *Cornigeri boves:* corned beef.
  iv. *Pax in bello:* freedom from indigestion.
  v. *De mortuis nil nisi bonum:* in the dead there is nothing but bones.

From French:
  vi. *Un Espagnol de forte taille:* a spaniel with forty tails.
  vii. *Je frappe: le sentinel ouvre:* I knock the sentinel over.
  viii. *La belle dame sans merci:* the girl friend who did not say 'Thank you'.
  ix. *Il jeta un coup d'œil à l'avis:* he threw a cup of oil at the bird.
  x. *Le peuple ému répondit:* the purple emu laid another egg.

Rather more rarely are howlers perpetrated in the opposite direction, but the following seem worthy of survival:

Band of Hope: *Orchestre d'Espoir*.
I do not know whether ... *Je ne sais pas mouton* ...
Match-makers: *fabricants d'allumettes*.
Stick no bills: *ne collez pas de becs*.

A relation or an extension of this group may sometimes be heard from the lips of a light-hearted linguist who intentionally maltreats his language. Mr F. E. Bailey recently recorded his use of the expression *ausgebraunt* for 'browned off', and was politely asked to improve it to *abgebraunt*; while E. Williams in *The Wooden Horse* has given us *blond genug* for 'fair enough'. Fit to be mentioned in such company is *Verkehrsmarmelade* for 'traffic jam'.

From these spontaneous ejaculations, which certainly lighten much ordinary conversation, a short step takes us to the transfusion of the humour of an original into an equivalent translation; but there are not many writers who can be funny in a language other than their own and instances are rarer. The greater, then, is the merit of Professor C. H. Carruthers, who put *Alice in Wonderland* into Latin, so that in *Alicia in Terra Mirabili* we may read, for 'Will you walk a little faster? said a whiting to a snail' the characteristically terse *'Paulo citius incede' sic alburnus cochleae*.

Our debt to the Professor was increased when he followed *In Terra Mirabili* with *Per Speculum*. This is particularly treasurable because philologists have so often seized upon the first stanza of 'Jabberwocky' and have used it to expound their ideas of the relationship between words and their meanings, so that the serious and the absurd, the scholarly and the inane, are mixed together in a refreshing pot-pourri.

> 'Twas brillig, and the slithy toves
>   Did gyre and gimble in the wabe,
> All mimsy were the borrogroves
>   And the mome raths outgrabe.

This becomes:

> *Est brilgum: tovi slimici*
> *In vabo tererotitant;*
> *Brogovi sunt macresculi,*
> *Momi rasti strugitant.*

The world of the mind is made richer by those who can contribute such imponderabilia.

As appears in Chapter XV, the translation of technical words and phrases has serious difficulties of its own, but when attempts are made to offload the burden to electronic computers a new opportunity for witticisms is created. One fears that the reported efforts of the machine are more likely to be fictitious than ever to have been seen on the output tape, but some of them are in themselves good enough to be preserved, while they serve to keep us in touch with the world of commerce. The following are among the efforts that have been in circulation:

   i. For 'The spirit is willing but the flesh is weak' one read 'The whisky is agreeable but the meat had gone bad'.

   ii. For 'hydraulic ram' we had 'aquatic male sheep'.

   iii. For 'Out of sight, out of mind' the transcript was 'Invisible, imbecile'.

These things are futilities, and to redeem the character of this chapter two first-rate examples may be given.

The first belongs to the genus of *abgebraunt*, and is told of Professor Richard Porson, one of the greatest classical scholars of all time. Returning to his rooms late one night, he found neither whisky nor candle in readiness, and carefully making his way across the floor he murmured, 'Οὐδέ τῶδε, οὐδε τἄλλα' (Oude tode, oude talla), the Greek phrase for 'Neither the one nor the other'.

Finally, there has never been a finer exploitation of a foreign language than Mr George Walker's account of an unsuccessful appearance on the cricket field. So many of us have recognized the saddening fact that an invitation from one's son's Headmaster to play in the annual Fathers' Match foreshadows the end of one's efforts at the wicket, that its very title evokes a nostalgia that adds to its value.

PAPA JOUE AU CRICKET

Papa joue au Cricket.
C'est une grande allumette – une deux-jour allumette.
Papa est dans le pré tout le premier jour.
Il laisse tomber deux attrapes,
    et manque trois balles dans le profond, qui vont à
    la borne pour quatre. Beurre-doigts!
Son capitaine le met sur à bouler. Il boule deux larges, et
    trois pas-balles. Il est frappé pour six. Il boule des
    plein-jets et des long-sauts et des demi-volées. Il est
    ôté. Il a l'analyse: – Pardessus, 3; Pucelles, 0;
    Courses, 38; Guichets, 0.
L'autre côté accourt une vingtaine de haute taille.
Papa s'assied dans le pavillon.
Il est dernier homme dedans.
Il regarde son capitaine, qui fait un siècle.
Après un premier-guichet debout, les guichets tombent.
Le filateur en prend quatre: un attrapé à court troisième
    homme, un dans le ravin, un autre à niais moyen-
    dessus, et le dernier vaincu par un qui va avec le bras.
Le marchand de vitesse fait le truc de chapeau parmi
    les lapins: un joliment pris à jambe-carrée, un dans
    les glissades, et l'autre battu et boulé tout au-dessus
    de la boutique.
Les joueurs courent. Le guichet-teneur casse le guichet.

178

Celui qui court n'est pas dans son pli. Il est couru
dehors.
Papa est dedans.
Il saisit sa chauve-souris.
Il marche à la poix.
Il prend milieu-et-jambe.
On boule. C'est un casse-jambe.
Papa ferme ses yeux. Il coupe en retard. Il manque.
On boule. C'est un Chinois.
Papa ferme ses yeux. Il accroche. C'est un coup de vache.
La balle lui frappe le genou. Le pré hurle, 'Comment
ça?' L'arbitre lève son doigt.
Cloches d'enfer!
Papa est dehors, jambe-devant-guichet.
Il n'a pas cassé son canard.
Hélas!

This is brilliant, unsurpassed and unsurpassable: to continue this chapter beyond it would be to introduce an
inevitable anticlimax which it were prudent to avoid.

XVII

Autonomy in translation

*To talk about translation is rather like talking about the glass in front
of a picture when it is the picture itself that engrosses our attention.*
J. LEHMANN

Lest the preceding chapter may have given an impression of
frivolity in what is essentially a serious and scholarly occupa-
tion, the intention of this last chapter is indeed to 'talk about
the glass', or in particular about the varied influences which
the glass may exert because of its existence.

To do this is in part to amplify the statement made in
Chapter IV to the effect that a translation is the product of
original thought and work by the translator. This gives
the translator an interest or a degree of ownership in his
translation, which is different from that of the author but
which undeniably exists. The translation belongs to the
translator in a way that it does not belong to the
author, and it is this creation of a new proprietorship
which gives to translating the autonomy that concerns us
here.

The autonomy derives from the basic fact, mentioned at
the beginning of this book, that several alternatives usually
exist for the translation of any one word in an original, and
the thesis that the choice between these alternatives raises
translating to the status of an art has, I believe, been justified.
But the very existence of alternatives puts both a responsibility and an opportunity before the translator, who can
choose the words that express his own opinions, or that of the
sect, company, or nation to which he belongs. In other words,
a translator can exploit the operation of translating so as to

support beliefs or theories in which the author may have held a contrary opinion.

An example will make the point clearer and, as always, the simpler the illustration the better it functions. I choose the few words: *Il me frappa sur l'épaule.*

In French there is a clear distinction between *battre* and *frapper* and in English there are several words that may be used as equivalents to the latter. But they are not equivalent among themselves, so that the translator has it in his power to determine the attitude of mind of the *frappeur*. He may write 'He tapped me on the shoulder' indicating that my attention was to be called to something; or 'He hit me on the shoulder', a blow of some force, perhaps, but not necessarily more than an accident: or again, 'He struck me on the shoulder', suggesting some degree of anger and aggression. All this shows how a translator may use, misuse or distort the process of translating, treading the narrow path between *suppressio veri* and *suggestio falsi*.

Autonomy in translation therefore means the power of translation to produce results and to create occasions which would not have existed in its absence. A few examples will demonstrate the varied nature of this power; and they can be chosen to range from the amusing and trivial to the significant and important.

The story of Saints Barlaam and Josaphat, told in Chapter III, is perhaps a borderline instance. Their names had been used in the original Greek story, but it was only in its translated form that the work became widely known and Barlaam and Josaphat became so popular as to achieve sainthood.

The richness of the English vocabulary is responsible for a misunderstanding that approached an international seriousness. In some small discussion between the Foreign Offices of Paris and Washington the latter had failed to make its position as clear as was desirable, whereupon a French newspaper printed the not unreasonable headline '*Nous demandons une explication*'. This was seized upon by the American Press who, quoting the four words in too literal a manner, proceeded to add an irate comment on the theme 'France *demands*; does she indeed?' Yet actually all that France had done was to *ask*, with all the courtesy common in diplomatic circles.

Scientists are not, in general, prone to worry about words or to quarrel about the expressions used by their colleagues in other lands, but on at least two rather well-known occasions they have been misled by imperfections in translation.

In 1869 the great Russian chemist Ivan Mendeleef published his famous generalization known as the Periodic Law. He wrote in Russian, a language with which the chemists of western Europe were then even more unfamiliar than they are today, and most of them came to learn of it through a German translation. Mendeleef had written a conclusion which might best have been translated, 'The elements arranged in the magnitude of their atomic weights show a periodic change of properties.' In the German the vital adjective was not given as *periodische*, but as *stufenweise*, or 'gradually', and this enabled some Germans to claim that this new idea was not Mendeleef's but had been previously published by Lothar Meyer. The faint controversy that arose is but seldom remembered today, but such argument as there was arose only because of the existence of translation.

A biological example has had more far-reaching effects. Jean B. Lamarck, the French zoologist, suggested in 1809 that a factor in evolution was the influence of the environment on the animal body, bringing about the structural changes that the body needed for adaptation to its circumstances. The word used by Lamarck was *besoin*, which should have been put to British readers as 'need', but which was, in fact, translated as 'want'. Thereupon the opponents of Lamarck tried to ridicule his theory, saying that he believed that an animal would produce a wing or a curved beak or a webbed foot merely because it wanted such an organ. The understanding consideration which Lamarck's work undoubtedly deserves was delayed by this imperfect paraphrase; and here again the progress of science was affected by an act of a translator.

Many who take no interest in scientific theories will be able to find comparable alternatives in different translations of the Bible. The Old Testament was written in Hebrew, a language in which opportunities for mistranslation are never far to seek, with the result that a translator, consciously or not, may so bend his choice of words that he may appear to support one particular doctrine at the expense of another. This has been called 'interpretive translation', and in cases where it affects men's faith it forms a genuine risk to translators who are inclined or even prejudiced towards one version as opposed to an alternative.

A quite mild example opens the very first chapter of the first book. Everyone knows that Genesis begins with the words 'In the beginning God created the Heavens and the Earth; and the Earth was without form and void ... ' In a translation to which we have already given some appreciative attention, the Goodspeed translation of 1927, we read 'When God began to create the Heavens and the Earth, the Earth was a desolate waste ... ' The implication of the second translation is that the Creation was not, in fact, the making of something out of nothing, but was a rearrangement and an ordering of something already in existence. Thus the translator has been able to steer his readers towards an acceptance of the view that he would wish them to take.

There is some reason to believe that the fate of Hiroshima was influenced by the fact of translation. After the Potsdam Conference an ultimatum was sent to the Japanese Government, demanding their surrender: their reply contained the vital word *mokusatsu*, the closest translation of which is to the effect that the answer would be delayed until discussion had taken place. But the translation received in Washington used the word 'ignore', the whole implication of which was very different. It must have strengthened the American resolve to drop the bomb.

This power of translation imposes a responsibility on the translator, who must accept it at the risk of being accused of bad faith. It extends to the reader of the translation, who may find it advisable to discover who has made the translation that is in his hands and something of his reputation for integrity.

NOTES

1. Finnish

Whatever may be the capacity of Greek to express the finer shades of thought or the capacity of German to serve as a satisfactory medium for its translation, the claims of another European language to a quality that challenges them both should not be overlooked. I refer to Finnish, a language that has but a small impact on readers in this country.

Finnish is a highly inflexional language, with fifteen cases, six persons and four moods, and this permits great variation in word-order with no obscuring of the sense but with the possibility of great variety in metrical stresses. It is even said that the hexameter is better suited to Finnish than to any other language.

Some readers may be interested to see Matthew Arnold's favourite six lines from the end of the Eighth Iliad put into Finnish:

> *Niin monet kuohuvan ksanthos-vuon välimaalla ja laivain*
> *troiast ulkona roihusivaj tulet iliolaisten.*
> *nous tuhat nuotiotulta, ja käynyt, kunkin ol ääreen*
> *viis' orokymment' istumahan tulen liekkivän hohtoon.*
> *ääress' ohrien kellerväin sekä selvien vehnäin*
> *vaunuillaan hevot kultaisen koin nousua vartoi.*

2. Caesar

In the first edition I had written, in translation of *propter altitudinem maris*, the words 'because of the depth of the water'. This is close to the Latin and is satisfactory to the mind of a scientist, subconsciously thinking of depth as a dimension which can be measured in fathoms or centimetres. But to the men in the Roman ships, as to anyone concerned in crossing a stretch of water, the feeling would be one of doubt and anxiousness, which I think is more nearly expressed by my revised phrase, 'because the water was so deep'.

3. Modern Languages

The contention that of the three modern languages usually taught in schools French is the hardest and Spanish is the easiest is so universally held by experienced teachers that its truth must be accepted. The differences may be expected to have an effect on the proportion of candidates who succeed in these languages in such examinations as those for the General Certificate of Education. Some interest therefore attaches to the following statistics extracted from the report of the University of London for the year 1966. The figures given are the percentages of candidates who passed.

	Secondary Modern Schools	Maintained Grammar Schools	Direct Grant-aided Schools	Recognized Independent Schools
French	43·5	69·2	80·7	78·4
German	57·1	66·3	85·2	63·9
Spanish	87·5	67·9	63·4	63·4

The anticipated order appears only in the Secondary Modern Schools: for the other three the average percentages of passes are French, 76 per cent, German 71 per cent, Spanish 70 per cent. These figures reverse the anticipated order, possibly because the harder a subject is found to be the greater is the effort that it calls forth from both teacher and pupil.

4. Russian

Nothing more than complete ignorance has forced me to omit all reference to Russian in the chapter on modern languages, realizing, as I do, that an ability to read the language is at present of rapidly increasing importance. This is especially true of science. As some compensation I record the fact that a translation of the *Odyssey* into Russian has been described by those who know it as 'very successful'.

5. Lalage

The different attempts to put the last two stanzas of Horace's Ode 22 into English verse were the most popular subject of the letters I received after the original publication of this book. Few of their writers refrained from sending me their own solutions to the problem, and one would wish for space in which to discuss them all. I limit myself to quoting two, with grateful acknowledgments.

The first is of interest because it was composed by a Dutch lady, who wrote, 'I dedicate it to the English language.'

> Where trees won't grow
> And coldly clouded skies
>   Oppress,
> Where heat bans life
> And fiercely scorching rays
>   Obsess,
> There shall I love
> The tender talk and smile
>   Of bliss.

> H. A. van Lier

The second was an exercise in word-economy; the author wrote, 'I swore an oath not to exceed thirty words.'

> On arctic upland
> No soft breeze,
> Gale and foul fog
> Blast stunted trees.
>
> On sun-baked sand
> No house, no herds:
> Your smile I love,
> And your soft words.

J. L. Synge

He adds, 'True, I don't mention Lalage by name, but then she was Horace's girl-friend, not mine.'

6. Omar Khayyám

While this book was being printed, Robert Graves's new translation of the Rubáiyát* was published and showed itself to be a work of combined scholarship and political ability that must mark it as one of the really great translations of the age. Unable at this late stage to write about it as fully as I should wish, I must content myself with a strong recommendation to my readers to study it and to notice the satisfying treatment of the stanza which I have discussed in Chapter XIII.

> In childhood once we crouched before our teacher
> Growing content, in time, with what he taught;
> How does the story end? What happened to us?
> We came like water, and like wind were gone.

* *The Rubáiyát of Omar Khayyám* by Robert Graves and Omar Ali Shah (Cassell, 1967).

INDEX